Dedication

My earliest memory is of my mother's smiling face. I was probably 3 or 4 years old, dancing in the living room with all 5 of my older siblings. The song playing was "love can't ever get better than this". I can hear the song in my head and I can see mom's face watching us dancing and laughing. My mom had long dark hair then, her big, warm smile and kind eyes gave me this overwhelming feeling I was loved. What better gift can a mother give her child than to know he is loved? My mother dedicated her life to her husband, her 6 children, her grandchildren, and her great grandchildren. Together with my dad, the two of them built an incredible legacy of love that is my family. She taught me everything from how to tie my shoes to how to be a good man. I am especially thankful she taught me how to pray and how to trust in the Lord. In the pages ahead I will take you through the journey that has been my life so far. A life I truly believe stems from the love of my Mother. My mother is at the core of who I am. I dedicate this book to her, Anita Louise (Simington) Sargent. No one encouraged me to write more than she did. I love you Mom.

Introduction

My name is Joe Rady. At the time of starting this book, I am 38 years old and I live in Madison, WI. I was born Joseph Donald Sargent, the youngest of 6 kids in a very small rural town in Northern Wisconsin. The area outside of town where we lived when I was very young was referred to as Mudbrook. Google isn't sure if Mudbrook is so much a town as it is a road, but to me and my siblings, Mudbrook was a very real place, with very vivid memories. Several miles outside of town, our house sat about 100 yards off the main gravel road. I recall back then there were no stop signs at the intersections of those gravel roads. Car seats, booster seats, even seatbelts were not something we bothered with. As the youngest of 6, my typical spot in the car was laying in the back window looking up at the sky. I would watch the dust clouds from the gravel roads being kicked up behind us as my dad drove us to wherever it was we were headed. Back then we were most likely headed to one of my siblings sporting events, one of my many aunts or uncle's homes, or church.

My parents are John and Anita, they married in 1975 and had 4 girls and 2 boys. My siblings in order are Marcy, Nick, Katie, Jenny, and Bobbi. I'm the youngest. When I was putting together the outline for this book, I considered telling more of their stories across the years as well, but as much as I loved being a part of them, they're not my stories to tell. You will hear all of them referenced many times throughout, but this is a collection of my life moments, and I won't try to do their life moments justice. Maybe someday each of them will write their stories for you. My sister Jenny is already a published author, so there's a chance! The following pages are a recount of my life so far. There's love, loss, life lessons, and laughter. I asked myself when I started this what it was I was hoping to accomplish. The truth is, from a pretty young age, I learned writing was cathartic for me. I enjoy it. Sometimes putting my thoughts and feelings and memories down on paper feels almost like a weight lifted. Like my mind can now free up space because I have everything saved on paper if I ever need it. My other hope is someone, somewhere, reads about my life, identifies with parts of it, and finds some kind of comfort in that.

Special thanks to my husband Jamie. I lost count of the number of times I shouted from our home office

"Hun, can you come here so I can read you this part?"

Without your support, patience, and encouragement, this book would never have come to fruition.
I love you.

Chapter 1
Population Unincorporated

Holcombe, Wisconsin. Let's call it "Mudbrook proper" for fun. I believe I was 5 when we made the few mile move from the Mudbrook house to Holcombe. The very definition of a small town. It's where I was born and raised and to this day, going back will trigger a flood of memories as I pull into town. The small strip mall on the right side of the highway is one of the first things you see right after the welcome sign declaring our Division 6 state football championship victory in 1998. The strip mall seems out of place because it wasn't there when I was a kid and has since been added after I left my little town. Everything else is pretty much exactly as I remember it.

As I make a left and head toward my old school I see the Lake Holcombe Café is still going with a parking lot full of cars. A small but very nice little place with a house attached to it. I don't know who owns it now but when I was a kid it was Jeff and Rhonda. My sisters used to babysit their kids and sometimes I would come along and help. I remember thinking it was neat to see inside the "house behind the scenes". I also remember a babysitting night that didn't go so well when one of my sisters put a frozen pizza in the oven along with the cardboard! Luckily no major harm was done.

On the next block right before the turn to the school is The Cheese House. It's sad to see it sitting there empty. When I was a kid, this was the place to go. Tiny and Sharon owned it then and I believe they have both since passed away. I don't know if I ever knew Tiny's real name and as a kid I didn't understand his nickname since he was a very big guy. I guess irony is something I learned later in life.

The cheese house, or "Casa de Queso" as my high school Spanish teacher would call it when we'd take our frequent field trips there, was a place that sold a little bit of everything. What I remember most about it though, was the ice cream! They had the BEST ice cream. I used to get rainbow sherbet as a kid and Tiny and Sharon would always smile at me and tell me how big and tall I was getting (spoiler alert, I was neither big, nor tall).

As a teenager, my frequenting of this place would be for reasons more than ice cream. My high school girlfriend lived with her family in the apartment above the store. She remains today a dear friend of mine. We don't see each other as often as I would like but we make the effort once a year or so to get together and we always have a lot of laughs when we do.

As I round the corner and up the street I pull into the big parking lot in front of a sprawling building. The elementary school sits, single story atop a small hill and is attached to the two-story high school built into the side of the descending hill. The memories that come racing back to me here as I close my eyes and sit in this parking lot are almost overwhelming. First of all, the building in front of me was not there when I was a kid. The school used to be much taller, 4 or 5 stories I think. I remember when they tore it down and redesigned it to what it is today. I was in between 3rd and 4th grade I believe.

New buildings or not, this particular space holds so much of my past. The Lake Holcombe elementary, middle, and high school are all one big building. To me, that's how school's worked because that's all I knew and I still find it odd when I drive through cities with one elementary school after another and multiple middle schools and high schools to choose from. My understanding was that school was the same building, same parking lot, same cafeteria, and gym for its entirety. From kindergarten plays on the stage to the day I walked across that same stage and accepted my diploma as a graduating senior, this was my school.

I remember the time a rather large kid on the playground came barreling down the big sledding hill at recess and collided into me. I was a "scrawny" kid who wouldn't hit 100 pounds until closer to high school. I knew I was scrawny because that's what countless people would call me and I always hated it. I spent the afternoon in the nurses office after that incident and it wouldn't be the last time I'd find myself there. For all the memories of injury or bullies though, I have just as many if not more of swing sets, monkey bars, red rover, jump rope, races to the white line on the tennis courts. I can close my eyes and smell the fresh cut grass and hear the sound the wood chips would make under my little shoes as I'd race to get the "good swing" at recess time.

In later years, the playground would mean less to me and I would begin to look for places that were more secluded where I could sneak away and smoke a cigarette. I was only 13 the first time I tried one, and by the age of 14 I was smoking pretty regularly. I remember smoking a cigarette more than once right here in this parking lot, in my little red 1985 Toyota Celica with the pop-up headlights. I loved that car so much! To clarify, I wasn't the "smokin in the boy's room, school sucks" type of kid at all. I actually did quite well in school. I enjoyed it, got along well with my teachers, and got good grades. Cigarettes were just that one thing I picked up and never should have that have followed me to this day.

I remember all my teachers. Most of the teachers I had as a kid have since retired and sadly a few have passed away. There's a stereotype that small public schools in rural towns don't provide as good an education as their counterparts in bigger cities. I certainly didn't find that to be the case. I was lucky to have learned from some of the smartest, kindest people I've ever known. I remember being struck in particular by the passion so many of them had for their career, for many better described as a calling than a career.

Mr. Mahalko was my 6th grade science teacher. That man was the definition of passionate. I've not met anyone, to this day who has described stars and constellations with more awe in his voice than Ken Mahalko. He had this awesome "star lab". A sort of giant inflatable sphere that we would all crawl inside and he'd hit the projector lights and it was like we were outside under the stars. He'd describe everything we were seeing with detail and excitement in his voice. I remember more than once driving past his house on our way to the next town over and seeing his ladder propped against his roof. He used to love to take his telescope up on his roof and gaze to the heavens. As I write this, I wonder if he still does.

Mrs. Randall, Mrs. Mataczynski now, was the music teacher... now there was a lady with passion! I remember fondly every moment in her classroom, from kindergarten to senior year. First of all, she could play the piano like nobody's business, and she could tear the roof off the place with her beautiful singing voice. It was her passion though that I remember most. She genuinely cared about her students. She was a hugger, a fixer of teenage drama, and a stand-in mamma for anyone who needed it.

Mr. Lanzer, Mrs. Kirkman, Mr. Meschievitz, all teachers I remember fondly. I believe my fascination with history started when I heard the way Ed Lanzer would describe events from our past. I remember him explaining that understanding where we came from can help us decide where we want to go in life. Mrs. Kirkman, the English teacher was a presence. Her brightly colored scarves, half glasses on a chain around her neck, her "queen of England" walk and talk and general royalty of presence. She was something else, but again, passionate. She and the music teacher partnered for years to produce and direct the school plays, the perfect duo for that job. Mr. Meschievitz was a large man with a small voice. He would suffer ridicule from so many kids, but the truth was that most of the kids really liked him. He was funny and quick witted. He was also the driving instructor for a long time. I remember learning to drive with him in the passenger seat offering up directions and reminding me to stop taking one hand off the wheel as I had a habit of doing. I heard of his passing a few years back and remember wishing I had been brave enough to tell him how well liked he was, I hope he knew.

There was the librarian, Mrs. Mahalko, one of several duos of married teachers at our school. She was my science teacher's wife, and she was a small and quiet woman who many kids thought was too strict with her library rules. To me, she was a friend. She let me use the best computer in the library to compose and print the many stories and poems I would write back then. More than that, she would proofread them for me and on so many occasions she would tell me I had a "real talent". Mary Mahalko encouraged me and made me feel good about my writing. As I sit here writing these words I find myself wondering what she'd think of my book. Teachers have more impact on the kids that pass through their doors than they will ever realize.

I sit in this parking lot looking at additional parking spaces where the detached agriculture building used to sit. I remember being in the back of that classroom, it was dark, and the projector was displaying a film strip on the wall. I was eating candy in class, which I wasn't supposed to do, but it was dark, and I figured I could get away with it. I was eating a gobstopper (which I haven't ventured to try again in over 20 years) when one got stuck in my airway. It was one of the scariest feelings I've ever experienced. Unable to breathe and in the dark unable to get anyone's attention, I began making noise by hitting the projector and disrupting the film. Mr. Guthman, the agriculture teacher, would realize something was wrong quickly and turn on the lights. He recognized what was happening and immediately performed the Heimlich maneuver on me. The piece of candy dislodged from my airway, and I was never more relieved in my short life than I was in that moment to be able to take a breath again. Years later, in my mid 20's I would write a letter to Mr. Guthman thanking him for saving my life and the letter I received back from him is something I store in a keepsakes box still today.

I have so many fond memories of growing up in that small town. I learned many life lessons there and made life-long friends. There would be times of triumph and times of heartache. I would learn everything from how to ride a bike to how to regain control of a car spinning out on snow covered roads. I would learn that not everyone would be ok with me just being me and that learning who I was myself would be an uphill battle all its own. I would learn later in life that the only real regrets are the chances I was too scared to take. Through it all, I had my great big family, a crew of hilarious, loving, amazing people that would be the primary guiding force in my life, shaping so much of who I would become.

Chapter 2
The Sargents

I think I was almost 12 years old the first time it ever occurred to me to ask my parents why my oldest sister, Marcy, was in their wedding photos. I had seen their wedding album plenty of times as a kid and even remember wondering why Marcy was the only one of us kids in the pictures. It's funny the things that "click" in our minds as we grow up.

My parents don't have the traditional "love story" of sorts, and for me, its honestly one of the things that helped me later in life. Knowing that something amazing can come from a story that's not perfect on paper is more powerful than the Hollywood "meet cutes" and romcoms I'd seen on tv. Dad was good friends with my Mom's younger brother Tony. Mom and my Dad knew of each other but were not actually dating. I don't know the whole story, but I do know that their pregnancy with their first child came along before any wedding proposal and Marcy herself came along a few months before their wedding. I never actually asked either of them if they got married just because of the baby because by the time I was old enough to wonder, it was already obvious to me that the answer didn't matter. My parents would go on to have 6 total kids and anyone that knew them at all could tell that they were head over heels in love with each other.

For most of my childhood, we lived on Dane road in rural Holcombe. Approximately 5 miles from the school, our house sat on 5 acres, one of only two houses on a dead-end road. Just over the hill was Isle Bay, a little inlet of access to Lake Holcombe. We could never have afforded to be "on the lake" people back then, but we were fortunate to live so close and we spent hours swimming in and fishing on that lake as kids. Our house was a mobile trailer home set behind a small addition of sorts that came with the property. Throughout my childhood we would have 3 different trailers on this same spot of land. The first two would be set behind the addition and the 3rd, a brand-new double- wide that I remember thinking was the fanciest thing ever, would be set next to it.

Dad, Nick, and I would build a connecting hallway in anticipation of the new home's arrival, and I believe the home is still set up that way as I write this. Mom and Dad sold it many years ago when all us kids were grown and moved out. It was a quiet little slice of heaven surrounded by pine trees and with a huge front and back yard. Dad would spend many years making constant improvements. From landscaping to the addition of a front porch, to an eventual 2 car garage. Between the ages of 5 and 18, all my important moments happened on that little dead-end road. I can close my eyes and see it so clearly, all my siblings out front on a hot summer day playing "what color's my birdie?". A ridiculous game in which one person would have a cup and be standing next to a bucket of water while the others shouted out colors until one of us guessed the color the holder of the cup was thinking. Whoever got it right would be met with a cup of water poured over their head, a welcome relief on a hot summer day. If you're not from Wisconsin or have never been there, you might picture a frozen tundra filled with snow. Make no mistake, Wisconsin summers get HOT, especially in the month of August. Some of the best days of my life were spent having water fights in that front yard with my siblings.

Marcy (pictured back right on cover), the oldest, was a born performer. She would strike a pose any time a camera was in front of her and from a very young age was already the "life of the party" type. She would land the lead role in her kindergarten play much to the surprise of my parents who say they showed up having no idea. She would learn early in life her talent for singing, she had the most beautiful voice, performing solos for concerts and competitions by the time she was in junior high. She was a very pretty girl with long auburn hair and a big bright smile. Somehow, she would end up the shortest one in the entire family. Neither Mom or Dad were very tall, Mom about 5'2" and Dad maybe 5'9". But poor little Marcy was barely 5 feet tall if that. In fact, I vaguely remember her driver's license having a disclaimer about needing some sort of booster to see over the steering wheel. Small girl with a gigantic personality, that was Marcy.

Nick (pictured back left on cover), kid number 2, was the original black sheep before I took over the title in the later years. He was a hilarious and hard-working kid, athletic, handsome and popular with lots of friends in school. The black sheep title would refer more to his struggles academically when measured against the rest of us. The Sargent kids had a reputation for doing quite well in school, but Nick always struggled. For a long time, it was thought that he just didn't like school or care about it, but we'd learn later in life that one of his primary struggles had to do with his inability to focus due to lack of sleep at night. As the one who shared a bedroom with him growing up, I can vouch for the fact that my brother never got a single night of actual restful sleep. His breathing was so bad and so loud that to this day I need some sort of noise in the background in order to sleep. In his adult years he'd see sleep specialists and today he has it much more under control. He and I were not very close when I was little. I always preferred to play with my sisters closer in age to me and I remember often feeling like I wasn't the little brother he had hoped for back then. He was so good at sports versus my one day in little league when I finally hit the ball and mistakenly ran to third base instead of first base. He was masculine and loved all things hunting, fishing, dirt bikes and such. I was often teased and called "prissy" or "sissy" by other kids back then, though despite our differences, if Nick ever heard someone make fun of me he'd have beaten them into dust. We were so different, and when you're young I guess it seems like that's a good reason not to be close. I am thankful that as we grew up, Nick and I would find out just how much we enjoy spending time together, despite our differences.

Katie (pictured center on cover), kid number 3, was and remains the planner of the family. Most families have one. The one everyone looks to for organizing anything and everything. Taller than her older sister but not by much, Katie was also a very pretty girl. Her hair was always long like Marcy's but much more bright orange than all the rest of us, a true redhead. She had a quality of determination from a very young age. Katie was one of those kids that was just sort of "born responsible". I wonder sometimes what that must have been like for her then and now. I can imagine it must be a burden a lot of the time. When I was little I remember thinking, why does she always get to be in charge when Mom and Dad are gone, while knowing full well the reason was obvious, it's just who she was. Katie did very well in school, had many friends, and by the age of 14 would already be dating the man she would spend the rest of her life with, build a family with, and I have no doubt grow old with. Katie may have been in charge a lot when I was little but most of my memories are of her making me laugh and making me feel loved. She looked out for me my entire life and continues to do so today. She has such strong intuition when it comes to her loved ones. She always knew and still knows if something is wrong or off with any one of us.

Jenny (pictured front right on cover) number 4, the tallest of the girls was still a shorty pants by most people's definitions. I think she made it all the way to 5'7". She had darker hair than all the other sisters and there are times I look at her and am in awe of her uncanny resemblance to our mom. A very pretty and vivacious kid, my sister Jenny would make many friends throughout her life. She would also spend hours reading books to me at night and using funny voices to make me laugh. She was and is one of the kindest and warmest people I've ever known. I can't tell you about Jenny without the chicken coop story (sorry Jen). I have no idea what it's like to be a middle child, but it's my understanding that there are a lot of times when it makes you feel unheard or unnoticed. Jenny and Katie sometimes struggled to get along when we were kids and I think their close proximity in age along with Katie often being left in charge were probably big factors. The chicken coop in our backyard would end up being where we'd find Jenny one afternoon after she'd hit her breaking point and announced she was running away from home. I don't recall how old she was, but I do recall feeling bad for her, in there crying, feeling all alone in the world. I wasn't much help as the littlest, not understanding much about emotions yet back then. I am glad she didn't make it past the chicken coop though, as I've continued to need her more times than I can count throughout my life.

Bobbi (pictured front left on cover) number 5, as it would turn out, would have a striking resemblance to Marcy, the oldest. With auburn hair of almost exactly the same color as Marcy's and another shorty, somewhere between Marcy and Katie in height I think, Bobbi was my sister that was closest to me in age, and all things really. We were less than a year apart, spending 5 whole days after my birthday but before hers each year reminding her I was the same age as her was one of my favorite past times as a kid. Bobbi was a bit of a tomboy. Often times filling the little brother role to my brother Nick better than I ever could. She was a savior for me. She liked to play with the girls and the boys. She never left me behind for either and would guide me on the latter when I was lost. She was popular and athletic and very pretty, the whole package. She would have many friends in school and lots of sports victories to celebrate. In her teen years, a car accident would leave her with some life-long shoulder pain that would make sports a lot more difficult. Like Nick, Bobbi struggled some in school, though she was more fortunate than Nick to learn the why earlier on. A mild case of dyslexia made schoolwork 10 times harder for Bobbi than it was for other kids. She had to work harder than everyone else to come up with her good grades. It seemed unfair, but she persevered and once she knew about the dyslexia was able to take advantage of a few different things that helped her. I vaguely remember a see-through red plastic thing that she'd place over the page of a book, turning all the text and the page to a reddish hue. I don't know if this is still a tactic used today, but back then it somehow helped the words appear less jumbled on the page for her and helped her focus. Bobbi was my go-to then for any and all things personal. I trusted her with all my secrets and leaned on her for support throughout my entire childhood.

Me (pictured front and center on cover, shirtless and with my shorts on crooked) the youngest of 6. I was and am a goofball at heart. I loved making my siblings laugh and still do. I had to fight hard to get a word in when I was little and being the resident comedian was my way of getting noticed. I knew from a very young age that I was not like most of the little boys my age, but it would be quite a few years before it really started to get to me. When I was little I was well liked by the girls and the boys in my life for the most part and it wasn't until that middle school age that my being different started to matter much. I spent countless hours as a child riding my bike, playing with my friend next door, doing whatever any one of my siblings was doing, most likely Bobbi, and many days at my mother's side in the kitchen watching her bake and learning that everything was better with a lot of butter. I would be told many times that I was overly sensitive, and eventually, later in life I would wear that accusation as a badge of honor, but it would be a journey filled with painful moments, heartache, and many life lessons. At the center of it all, I was a Sargent, and I maintain that being a member of this family will always be the greatest blessing I've ever had.

Chapter 3

Things Mom Would Say

I remember once when I was 5 years old, my mom was putting my little fall jacket on me while we waited for the school bus to arrive to take me to my 2nd or 3rd week of kindergarten. I was telling her about a kid at school who was weird, and nobody sat with him at lunch.

As she knelt down and zipped my jacket closed, she looked at me with this very serious face and said, "you need to be friends with that boy". When I asked her why she said, "because you have a big heart, and when God gives someone a big heart, they have to use it to be kind to lots of people."

Now it wasn't at all uncommon for my mother to say things like this throughout my childhood and my entire life, but who knows why certain things stick with you more than others. For some reason, those words just burned into my little brain... I actually remember thinking my heart was physically bigger and feeling this sense of newfound responsibility toward anyone hurting. I don't remember what age I was when I first realized my heart wasn't actually physically bigger but I'm sure I had that moment. What I do know looking back is that those words from my mother quite literally shaped me into the person I am today. I'm not perfect, I've made mistakes, but I can say with confidence that I've tried very hard all my life to be kind and compassionate to others.

I don't know if my mother actually thought I was overly compassionate already at 5 or if she just said those words to inspire me in that direction, but it doesn't really matter. What matters is that I never, ever forgot what she said to me that day and even as I grew, and my understanding of what she meant evolved, I still continued through life with the belief that I was destined to be kind and considerate and helpful to others.

As a result of this conversation, I made some really wonderful friends in my early years. I tried to consider their feelings as much as possible and often had teachers and aunts and uncles tell me I was "wise beyond my years". I used to love hearing that... turns out once you reach a certain age it's just expected, so that ship sailed a while ago, but I still have fond memories of feeling "adultier" than my young counterparts.

I remember this one time I had checked out a book from the school library that was all about manners and etiquette. All the other kids were reading Judy Blume books or Goosebumps or whatever was trendy, but I loved this little red book about manners. I remember bringing it home and trying out one of the first things in it at the dinner table with my family. I placed my little napkin gently across my lap, kept my elbows off the table, waited my turn to dish items onto my plate, and said please and thank you with every interaction. I think my brother called me something along the lines of a dingus and one of my sisters called me a suck up, but I was loving this new world of politeness and courtesy that I had discovered in my little book.

It's strange to think that I took some of the lessons from that book with me all the way through my entire life to present day. Good manners and general politeness are a part of who I am. I wonder if the book resonated with me because that's who I was or if who I am was shaped somewhat by my fascination with that book. I wish I could remember the name of it, would be such a kick to read it again more than 3 decades later.

Chapter 4

Watered Down Truths

I very clearly remember the first time I ever got to have a sleep over at a friend's house. I was so excited all day knowing I would be going over to his house, especially since he'd told me in school all the cool stuff he had that we could play with! My friend, we'll call him Sam, lived not far from my house and I knew from riding the same bus that his house looked really big and really nice compared to mine. I always got on the bus before him in the morning and off the bus after him in the afternoon, so he'd never seen my house. I remember a debate when we were cooking up the idea of asking our parents about a sleepover on who's house we'd choose. I pretended to protest a little when he suggested his house but secretly hoped that'd be the result, I was so curious what it was like inside.

After school that day I was bursting with excitement. When the bus pulled up to Sam's house, instead of waving my usual goodbye, I raced off the bus right along with him and toward his house. Looking back, I have to wonder if our parents mentioned this plan to the bus driver or if he just assumed it was fine. It was a very small town in the late 80's so the latter is totally feasible. I remember coming through the front door and Sam immediately insisting that we go see his room first. I thought it was pretty cool that he had a room of his own. I'd only ever shared with my brother at this point in life. He had a big bed and a HUGE collection of toys. There were Legos and Tonka Trucks and model airplanes, you name it. I lost interest immediately in exploring the rest of his house as we settled onto his bedroom floor and let ourselves get lost in whatever make believe world we would come up with.

Sam and I were in the middle of expanding the Lego zoo we'd been constructing to include a lion den when we heard his Mom call us for dinner. Sam was reluctant and didn't want to quit playing but I remember I was hungry as it was quite a bit later than when my family usually ate. We made our way to the dinner table and his Mom told us to go wash up first. When we returned, Sam's older brother and sister were at the table and so was his Mom, we took our seats and I remember looking around a little confused as to why there was no food on the table and there didn't appear to be anything in the kitchen waiting to be moved to the table either. It was then that the patio door behind me slid open and in walked Sam's Dad with a big plate of burgers he'd just prepared on the grill outside. I don't believe at this time that we had a grill at my house and I remembered thinking this was a really neat experience.

As the burgers and sides were passed around and everyone was fixing their plate, I waited patiently for my turn with the ketchup. When it was finally in my hands, I squirted some out onto my plate and immediately stopped, wide eyed and concerned. I turned to Sam and whispered that something was wrong with it. He quickly inspected the ketchup on my plate and his own then looked inquisitively at the bottle and said, "what's wrong with it?". I was polite to a fault and I didn't want to be rude or cause any sort of issue so I continued in my whisper tones and explained to Sam that the ketchup was dark red and thick and stayed in one little blob on my plate when I squirted it out. He continued to look at me confused, waiting for me to say something that sounded like a problem with the ketchup but clearly he wasn't hearing one yet. Finally Sam said, "that's how ketchup is supposed to be, just try it".

I gave up my protest and decided to try it. It was good, tasted mostly the same as the ketchup I was used to at home but just looked so different. At home, my ketchup was always lighter in color and a little watery and would usually spread out on the plate a lot more. It would be quite some time later in life before I would discover that sometimes to make ends meet, my mother would water down our ketchup at home to make it last longer.

After dinner Sam and I raced back to his room to play some more and continued to do so for the entire evening until his mother insisted it was time for bed. The next morning before school, Sam's mom was asking his older siblings what they wanted for breakfast when Sam and I walked into the kitchen. I remember his siblings looking at several different brightly colored boxes and trying to make a decision. Sam sat down at the table so I joined him and his mother brought us each a bowl and spoon and then sat down a box with a brightly colored bird on the front and told me this was Sam's favorite and asked if I wanted the same. Again not wanting to be impolite I said sure then quickly whispered to Sam, "what is that?" He quickly replied that it was something called Fruit Loops. I didn't realize his mom was close enough to hear us and was startled when she said from behind me, "You've never had fruit loops??". I remember feeling a little embarrassed, like this was something I should have known about but not only had I never heard the term fruit loops, I couldn't recall having ever seen cereal in brightly colored box before. At my house, cereal came in giant oversized clear bags, usually with words like price busters or food mart on the side and generic names like fruit rings or corn puffs.

When Sam poured the fruit loops into his bowl I remember exclaiming loudly "Oh FRUIT RINGS!" At the time, I didn't completely understand why this made his mom laugh so hard, but looking back I certainly do. By this point in my first sleepover I was starting to get the hint that perhaps it wasn't Sam's life that was so unique, but rather mine. I honestly didn't ever really realize prior to this that my family struggled financially when I was a kid. I was so used to the way things worked in my house that I thought that was how it was everywhere. I decided this was not the right time to mention how thick the shampoo was that I used in their shower that morning. Another thing it turns out my mom would sometimes water down at our house.

Looking back on this time it makes me laugh to think how small my world was. I think about how narrow my frame of reference was on everything and I realize how important it is to broaden one's horizons, travel, see the world, experience other cultures. As children, we're expected to know the world only through our limited experiences, but as we grow, I believe we have a responsibility to ourselves and to each other, to learn more, see more, experience more. Otherwise, we'd all end up thinking our cereal, our ketchup, and our shampoo were the "right" ones and everyone else's are wrong. A simple misunderstanding at a young age but a huge life lesson for me as I'd grow.

More than just a life lesson on the different life experiences of different people, moments like these in my childhood, as it turns out, would come in handy years later. Learning that your parents had to make money stretch and find creative ways to make ends meet can be jarring when you're a child, but as so many things do, this experience would eventually come full circle for me. Understanding hard times and how to persevere within them was a gift from my parents that I didn't recognize as such until much later in life.

Chapter 5

Megan, Marcy, and Miki

I will never forget my interaction with one of my absolute best friends, Megan Ralston, when she confronted me one day in the 3rd grade about my oldest sister (age 16 at the time) being pregnant with her boyfriend's baby. Now I knew my sister Marcy was pregnant. Mom and Dad had sat us all down a few weeks before and told us the news that Marcy was going to be having a baby. I remember being so incredibly excited. After all, I was the youngest of 6, I never got to experience what the other 5 did... a younger sibling to boss around and be smarter than, bigger than, faster than. Granted I was 9 years old at this point and I was smart enough to know that babies aren't much fun until they start walking and talking, but I was still excited anyway.

Another reason I was excited was that I had a natural caretaker type of quality. More common in girls my age, playing with dolls and pretending to be their mommies. I didn't play with dolls much but I did like the idea of holding a baby and making a baby fall asleep in my arms. By this age, I knew better than to mention that to too many people. I already knew almost everything about me was different from the other boys in my class so I tried not to give them more reasons to make fun of me.

Back to my confrontation with Megan. Now understand, Megan and I were and are friends. This type of interaction was not her bullying me or us fighting, we just had the kind of friendship where we didn't hold back our thoughts and feelings with each other. I loved Megan for her friendship and her honesty. She was standing there, hand on hip, asking me to explain why my 16 year old unmarried, high school student, sister had sex with her boyfriend. This got the attention of a lot of other kids so now our discussion had a bit of an audience. Now I should tell you that one of the other unique things about me at this age was my uncanny ability to argue a point like a corporate attorney (my teachers HATED that) completely regardless of whether I was right, wrong, or had any facts whatsoever. I can't tell you why I believed what I said because I genuinely don't remember where on earth I got this idea but I do very clearly remember putting Megan in her place and teaching most of my 3rd grade class that "You don't HAVE to have sex to get pregnant Megan! My sister would never do that! Pregnancy is just an exchange of body fluids between a guy and a girl. If you kiss long enough your DNA mixes up enough to cause the girl to become pregnant!".

I remember Megan standing there stunned along with most of the rest of my class. The stunning part to me looking back on it was how quickly everyone just bought what I said. Now mind you, I really believed what I was saying so I am sure that helped sell it, but no one questioned me. Not one kid said I don't think that's true... they just stood there in awe and terror of this new revelation. I believe that was the moment I first thought perhaps I should become a lawyer someday (spoiler alert, I didn't).

I don't recall when I discovered the truth about how my sister got pregnant. I think that standard video they make you watch about the birds and the bees was in 5th grade but I am pretty sure I figured it out before that. What I do recall is the first time I held my niece in my arms. July 7th, 1992, my little Miki was born. Mackenzie Renee, Miki for short. That first year of her life, she lived at home with the rest of us and I recall it to this day as one of the most love filled and amazing times of my life. I loved growing up in a big family but having it get even bigger, if only for a short time...well, the walls of our little house were bursting, we all fell in love with her so quickly.

I am sure Marcy's story of events would include a lot more drama than mine. I am sure she was scared and I know she faced some ridicule from the other kids at school. But as the 9 year old littlest brother, most of what I remember from that time was the countless hours I spent making Miki laugh. Her little baby laugh was the most amazing thing in the world to me and it's how I spent most of the first year of her life, finding new ways to make her laugh. Turns out it would become a pattern that shaped our relationship for years to come, she's nearly 30 now and just this morning we were exchanging hilarious TikTok videos of animals being dubbed over by human voices. Our humor is one and the same. If something makes me laugh and no one else, I send it to Miki because I know she'll crack right up. I cherish my relationship with her.

Miki and I in Columbus, OH in the summer of 2011. I have tons of more recent pictures of the two of us, but I look really thin in this one and it's my book so I get to pick the photos.

Chapter 6

Jake and the *Dad* Man

I was devastated when Marcy graduated and announced that she and Miki and TJ (Marcy's boyfriend and Miki's dad) would be moving 3 hours away to the other side of the state. I was old enough to understand that this would be coming, but I wasn't prepared for it to be so far away. In my mind I always secretly assumed when she moved out that it would be close by. In my best dreams I pictured the 3 of them building a little house right in our backyard, though I knew that one was probably a stretch.

Over the next few years Marcy and TJ would put down roots 3 plus hours away from the rest of us and work hard to build their little family. If I remember right, TJ proposed with Miki on his knee and said "will you marry us" instead of "will you marry me". I always thought that was the sweetest thing. I remember wearing my little tux to serve as an usher at their wedding, a job I took very seriously. It was also the first time I ever wore a tux and I very distinctly remember loving being dressed up in fancy clothes and shoes. I type this while looking over at my open hall closet overflowing with every color of dress shoe imaginable.

In the spring of 1995 I became an Uncle for the 2nd time. Marcy and TJ welcomed their 2nd child, Jacob John. Such a cute little thing, and Miki was over the moon about him. She vowed from the first day she ever held him to be his life-long protector. She has played the role of big sister extremely well all these years, her little bro adores her and she him.

I remember watching TJ transform during this time from the Metallica t-shirt wearing, long shaggy hair, free spirit kid type to the responsible "Dad man", take care of my family type. He loved his wife and kids and it became very important to him to provide well for them. This is another one of those moments where I am sure Marcy's book or TJ's book would have a whole lot more to say. I understand looking back but didn't at the time. They were so young, started a family before they were even out of high school, thrust into adulthood so quickly. I can imagine there were some pretty tough times between them, but I know they loved each other.

I remember the first time we journeyed as a family the long drive over to see their new apartment. I remember thinking it was such a LONG trip at the time, but being so excited when we pulled into the Fox Run apartment complex and getting to spend a couple days at their place.

My favorite though was when they would come home to visit. I remember this big old brown boat of a car that they had with a trunk bigger than most of the cars on the road nowadays. Marcy used to pack that trunk full of every single thing her kids could ever possibly need for the weekend and then some. Oh how I loved when that car would pull up. Racing out to get Miki and Jake out of their car seats and hug them up and listen to them squeal as they ran for the house toward my parents (Granny and Gramps to them).

It's so strange to think that I was living some of the very best days and memories of my life and not knowing it at the time. I am forever grateful for those days and how much simpler life was then, for me anyway.

Chapter 7

Dad

I have so many different memories of times spent with my Dad as a kid. While there are a handful of awkward moments where I felt like we didn't really understand each other, the truth is, the majority of my memories include so much laughter. To understand my Dad you need to know that he is the reason I make it my sole mission in life to make others laugh. The man was constantly cracking us up when we were kids. I have so many memories of him making my Mom laugh too. I remember around the time when Facebook was first becoming popular, sitting in the living room at my sister Katie's house. Her kids were little then and there were a lot of little kid books within reach of any spot in her house. Dad was sitting on the couch next to Mom, who was in conversation with one of the kids when he started poking her arm and saying "Nita, Nita, Nita", she finally turned toward him and exasperatedly said "What?!", at which point he picked up one of the kids little books, placed it against his cheek and said "Facebook" followed by his trademark chuckle. My Dad was the king of "Dad jokes" but also always had a very quick wit and always had a way of making any situation into a reason to laugh.

Something else you should know about him is that he could find a use for just about anything. He was very creative and he was never "above" anything. Dad never took himself too seriously and while I am sure he had his moments like anyone, most of what I remember from my younger years were countless adventures and ideas, many of which from the outside looking in might have seemed crazy, but I consider myself so blessed to have grown up in an environment like that, where no idea is a bad idea and with a Dad who had an attitude that I can only describe as "why not? Let's give it a shot?!"

There was the time the shifter on his old truck broke, causing it to be stuck permanently in reverse. Dad still found ways to make good use of it. Many a days I can remember hearing that familiar "eeeeee" sound of a vehicle in reverse and I would look out the back patio window to see Dad hauling brush or firewood in that old truck. He'd back up to whatever he was loading up then continue in his only option of reverse, sometimes backing over whatever else was in his path and making a wide circle to head back the other direction.

I remember him talking when I was a kid about wanting a convertible one day. I will never forget the time he bought an old car and decided to make his own convertible. I remember watching him with some sort of large power tool hacking away at the roof of that old car and eventually successfully cutting the top right off. I remember pointing out to him that not being able to put the roof back on made it more of a "converted" than a "convertible", which we both laughed at. I also remember we didn't have a garage at that time and will never forget the "oh shit" look on his face when he came in the house after removing the roof of the car and Mom asked him what he planned to do when it rained.

I suppose looking back that it could be said that My Dad had a tendency to be overly impulsive from time to time, and it's not at all lost on me that I inherited this trait from him. That said, what great story ever starts with "after 6 months of careful consideration and thoughtful deliberation…" Who wants to read that book?! I admit freely that being impulsive is not always a good thing, but growing up with a Dad that often threw caution to the wind, had big ideas, and was by all accounts a dreamer at heart would set me up for a lifetime of adventures, all of which I am incredibly grateful for. I spent many days of my youth in that backyard with my Dad, riding in the back of a truck that only went in reverse, helping him with various projects, and one time flying out of the bed of the truck when he backed it into a tree. How I never broke any bones is still a mystery to me, but what I remember most is the laughter. I will forever be grateful for a Dad that always found a way to make everything fun.

Me and Dad, June of 2014. He looked so handsome in his tux

Growing up in a big Irish catholic family was pretty common in northern Wisconsin. Mine was certainly not the only one. I had a lot of friends that I would see in school all week and also in church on Sunday. I remember Sundays well, I can tell you where every one of my aunts and uncles sat in church every Sunday, everybody always had the same pew.

My Grandma Simington (mom's mom) always sat in the very first row right up front. She always wore a tight fitting little hat and would often be wearing something red, her (and my) favorite color. Behind her would sit her oldest daughter, my Aunt Judy, and her husband Gary and before their kids were grown and moved away there'd have been 5 children in the pew next to them. Uncle Mark and Aunt Kim and their 3 kids would be one pew back and off to the left side with Aunt Sue and Uncle Earl and their 3 kids a row or two behind them.

We always sat about halfway up on the left side, I remember it was close enough to Sue that I was usually able to see her and her kids best throughout the service. I can't remember for the life of me where

Aunt Phyllis and Uncle Kurt sat but I think that's because they ended up getting so heavily involved in the church that I have more memories of them participating in the service in some way. Uncle Kurt is a Deacon now in fact.

Sundays were one of my favorite times, not because of church, truth be told I always found it a bit boring as a kid. My favorite part of Sundays was that after church we would almost always gather with all my mom's side at either Sue's, Phyllis's, Judy's, Mark's or our house and I would get to spend the day playing outside with all my cousins. Most often we ended up at Phyllis's house, likely because she lived just up the street from the church we all attended. I remember I used to be scared of her balcony that overlooked her living room down what seemed like, to a little kid like myself at the time, a thousand feet and 100s of stairs down. I remember seeing it again as an adult after not having been there in many years and realizing just how few stairs there were and how it was not nearly as intimidating as I had remembered.

Back in those days as a kid on Sunday's after church, I would put aside my balcony fears and we would all spend hours playing in that living room or the backyard. Mom and her sisters would usually be visiting and making something for lunch for everyone while Dad and Mom's brothers and brother's in law would be discussing the latest topic of interest and often playing cards. Those were some of my favorite times as a kid, all of us together like that every Sunday.

On the occasion we gathered at Uncle Mark's I almost always got myself into some sort of predicament. Uncle Mark's house was on the dairy farm my Mom grew up on. Mark had taken it over when Grandpa died and Grandma lived in a trailer just up the lane now, not far from the house where she'd raised her kids with Grandpa Paul. Mark would start his family and raise his kids there and today his youngest is married with kids and carrying on the same tradition.

I absolutely loved when we'd go out to the farm, but I was the furthest thing from a "farm kid". I loved it because of the freedom, there was so much space to play and run around. There was almost always a fresh batch of newborn kittens and my favorite was when there were newborn calves. I loved playing up in the hay loft, my cousins had a rope swing up there and it was so much fun, except for the time I misjudged and plummeted in between several stacks of hay. There was also the time I was hurrying out of the barn because I heard my Mom calling for me and I ran out the "wrong side". In my defense, I didn't know there was a "wrong side", but that's a mistake you only make once. I never did get my shoes back from that manure pit after Dad pulled me out.

Aunt Sue's house was just up the road from the farm and Aunt Judy's was right across the road. Aunt Judy always had the best sweet treats and I remember her carpet in her living room being so soft it made you want to lay down on it and take a nap. Aunt Sue's was fun because I think her family was the first ones to get a trampoline, we jumped on that thing for hours! I remember being obsessed with my little cousin Kelly back then, Sue's youngest. She was a year or two older than me and I wanted to be just like her. She was smart and funny and a little sassy and I remember thinking she was cool. Unfortunately, she didn't appreciate my being enamored with her very much and I remember her saying to me on many occasions in an exasperated little voice "Stop following me around!" Poor Kelly, I tried so hard to be her shadow and it drove her right up the wall. Today she is an accomplished medical professional, mother, and cancer survivor. I still find her to be cool and sassy but now I also find her to be inspirational, plus she rarely ever tells me to stop following her around anymore.

It was always kind of a treat when the gatherings would end up at our house. All my cousins lived in the same general area and we were the only one's that lived the next town over so it was more of a drive for everyone to come to our place. Nevertheless, sometimes they did and I would get to show my cousin Billy the latest cool toy I had or the fort I built in my backyard. I remember most of my childhood we had a volleyball net set up in our yard and to this day gatherings of my family almost always include rousing matches of volleyball, one of the few sports I actually enjoy playing.

As I got older and so too did my cousins, the big Sunday gatherings would become more and more rare. Everyone got busy with their own lives and eventually the kids were getting married and starting families of their own. I look back on those days fondly and think of my cousins often. I don't see them nearly as much as I would like, but with social media these days, I at least get the occasional glimpse into their lives, see pictures of their kids and now even some of their grandkids. I may not have gotten a ton out of church itself, for me I was always more comfortable talking to God in my own quiet moments or when out in nature, but the times we spent together as a big extended family in those days created memories for which I will always be grateful.

Chapter 9

The Lake House

My Dad's side of the family was more spread out. His brother, My Uncle Dave lived just one town over from us with my aunt Cindy and their sons Jason and Jake. Dad's two sisters, Lenny and Vickie lived further. Lenny in a suburb of Chicago, IL and Vickie a suburb of Denver, CO. Gatherings with Dad's side were more rare but boy did we have a lot of fun when we did get together. My Aunt Lenny and Uncle Bob along with their two kids Justin and Whitney owned a 2nd home on the lake not far from where I grew up. Almost every summer they would host a big gathering out at their lake house. Aunt Vik and Uncle Rick and their two kids Jessie and Chelsea would fly in from Colorado, Uncle Dave and family would be there, and then my family would arrive, the big ole family of 8! Grandma Lois was always there (Dad's mom). She was one of the sweetest people I'd ever known in my life and I adored her.

I remember loving everything about that lake house. From the long driveway, to the house itself which had a cool layout and lots of toys that my cousins would let me play with. There was this old silo in the yard for some reason and as a kid I remembered thinking it was

500 feet tall! Then there was the lake just steps from the house. It was a great place to gather and I have many great memories there.

Seeing Dad's side less often meant longer talks when we did get together and more to catch up on. I can remember talking my poor Aunt Vickie's ear off every time I would see her. She was so much like her Mom, my grandma Lois, kind and funny and so very warm. She used to make me feel like everything I did and said was special and important, probably why every time I saw her it was like a moth to flame, who doesn't love a person that makes them feel like that?!

I remember also that the lake house would be the place where I would sneak my first sip of beer and the place where I would try my first puff of a cigarette. I remember hating both at the time, a problem I wish I still had today. I remember one particular summer one of my Aunts choked on something and the other saved her with the Heimlich maneuver. For some reason I can't recall which was which anymore, but what I do recall is them spending the rest of the weekend repeatedly singing wind beneath my wings hitting the "did you every know that you're my hero" part hard. There was always a lot of laughter with gathering on the Sargent side and I loved when Dad and his siblings would get going on stories of their childhoods.

I remember one in particular, and if you're reading it that means I clarified some of the details from my Dad to make sure I got it right. As I recall, Dad and his brother Dave once poured lighter fluid on their arms, lit them on fire, and rode a horse past their picture window while flailing their "burning" arms to scare their mom! I believe there was another story about Dad and his sister Vickie secretly trying out curse words by saying them to each other and Vickie spilling her guts at the dinner table because the guilt was eating her alive. Dad and his siblings have so many stories and as a kid I used to love just sitting around the campfire by that lake and listening to them all sharing and laughing together.

Looking back it makes me realize how much I miss what was a much simpler time. There's an innocence to life when you're young and a sort of wide-eyed naivety that nothing bad will ever happen to you or your family. We lost my cousin Jake a few years ago to a snowmobile accident. Life changes fast, the memories you make when you are young become so important and you realize how much you hang onto them later in life. I miss those simpler times so very much.

Chapter 10

The Summer of '97

I spent a lot of my weekends and summers with my best friend Josh. He was the boy next door. Keep in mind this was before social media and internet, back when I was little, most kids met and became best of friends based on the proximity of their houses. Josh didn't actually live next door to us, his Grandparents did, but he was there all the time and so was I. They had this wonderful little hobby farm with chickens, ducks, donkeys, even a potbelly pig and a fox at one time! While the close proximity helped launch our friendship, our shared sense of humor and mutual enjoyment of animals and being outdoors is why it stuck I think. My sister Bobbi often joined us and the three of us would spend hours playing the hunter and the wolf, or feeding the chickens, or swinging on the old metal swing set in the yard next to the duck pond. Fun fact, that boy next door is now my brother-in-law, married to my sister Bobbi, they have 6 kids, the oldest of which just moved out of the house and got married. The paths life takes us on are truly incredible. I can remember being on that swing set, the 3 of us, like it was yesterday.

There was one particular summer in which Bobbi and I didn't see Josh nearly as much though. It was the summer of 1997. My sister Marcy and her husband and two kids were still living across the state and working hard to make ends meet. Marcy had invited Bobbi (15 at the time) to live with her for the summer and provide childcare for the kids during times of overlapping work schedules for her and TJ. Bobbi agreed and went to live with Marcy for the summer. A couple of weeks in Bobbi got sick (I think it was strep throat, hard to remember anymore). I volunteered to go stay for a week or so and help with the kids until Bobbi got better. Bobbi got better quickly but my week stay turned into the entire summer. Bobbi and I watched the kids together and spent the entire 3 months re-bonding with our sister Marcy. I recall a lot of laughter that summer. The time Marcy tackled me into the full kiddie pool in my church clothes just because she thought it would be funny. The time Bobbi and I rode our bikes into town and stopped to climb a rock wall, which I fell all the way down and Bobbi had to piggy back carry me all the way back to the house.

Oh the time Marcy and I were shopping and had a bit of an incident with a bottle of scented carpet powder. My sister Marcy, you have to understand, when she laughed, would lose all ability to do anything... like stand up, not pee her pants, communicate with other humans in anyway. I will never forget being covered in powder in the check out aisle and the cashier asking if everything was ok as I shook my head and carpet powder flew from my hair all over the conveyor belt and Marcy lost it all over again.

Coming home and starting high school was hard for me. All I really wanted to do was be back at my sister's house, watching the kids and laughing a LOT. She also let me smoke cigarettes when I was there and Mom and Dad were NOT having it when I got back. I never actually asked her if she got in any trouble for that, but I know I sure did. Though it still didn't stop me from smoking in secret. Really wish I'd never picked up that first cigarette. I am still a pack a day smoker. I keep saying I will give it up someday, but it's not today.

Life carried on, Marcy still came to visit a lot and I was adjusting to high school. My friend Josh's grandma got sick and we lost her to cancer right around this same time frame, she was so young, only in her mid 50's. He was devastated of course, as was I, she was always so kind and wonderful to me and it felt like losing my own grandmother. I miss her dearly still and think of her often.

Chapter 11

The Last Photo

Halloween 1997. I was so excited when I answered the phone a few days prior and it was Marcy on the other end. She said she wanted to bring the kids for the Halloween weekend and take them trick-or-treating. She said TJ would be up north hunting and asked if I would go along trick or treating and help her with the kids. I loved spending time with Marcy and the kids so much so I didn't have to hesitate on my quick answer of yes.

Friday night, October 31, we headed out. Miki dressed as a Unicorn and Jake in a ridiculously oversized pumpkin costume. We stopped at every house in the little town and laughed until our sides ached when Jake told an old lady to smell his feet. We stopped by our Aunt Phyllis's house as one  of our last stops and she had us all pose for a picture.

On Saturday, November 1, 1997 (All Saints Day), a call came into the house around 7pm. Marcy had been at a birthday party for her husband's cousin being held in town at a local hotel bar and restaurant. She had gone to the store and on the way back there'd been an accident. The car rolled, they estimated, as much as 6 times. I remember my parents racing out of the house to meet the ambulance at the hospital. Back at home waiting to hear word on her condition were myself, my sister Bobbi, Josh, my sister Katie, my cousin Stacey, and Marcy's kids, Miki, and Jake (ages 5 and 2 at this time). My brother Nick was hunting up north with Marcy's husband TJ and my sister Jenny was at the movies with her new boyfriend Keven.

The closest emergency room was more than 30 minutes away so we expected Mom and Dad to be gone awhile before we got a call from them with any updates. When the front door opened and it was Mom and Dad walking back in already. I remember being very confused as to why they were back so quickly. I don't recall if either of them actually said anything but I do recall my Mom having a shocked look on her face and my Dad just dropping to his knees and beginning to weep uncontrollably. It was one of the single most difficult moments of my entire life. I remember everything around me suddenly seemed to be in slow motion. My memories of that night play out like a movie that I was watching from afar instead of experiencing up close.

Miki was so concerned by all the tears and so smart for her age that she demanded to know what was going on. I think it was my sister Katie who finally summoned the courage to do her best to tell Miki that her Mommy wouldn't be coming home. There's nothing quite so heart breaking and gut wrenching as watching a child learn that their mother died. Jake was too little to completely understand but I remember him repeating to everyone for weeks after "my mommy died". He didn't really know what it meant but he knew it was making everyone sad and he was probably still wondering when Marcy would be joining the rest of us at the house. My heart ached for my little niece and nephew and part of it still does today. It's been almost 25 years and there isn't a day that goes by that Marcy isn't in my thoughts.

Chapter 12

Emotional Walls and Steel Guardrails

The weeks that followed Marcy's passing were a blur. The number of people that came out to pay their respects at her wake was astounding. The line of people stretched out the door and into the street. "She was so young and so full of life". "What will those poor kids of hers do without their mama". A seemingly endless parade of people each saying pretty much those same two things. I remember standing outside the funeral home at one point smoking a cigarette (I was 14 at the time) and not one person questioning me for it. I remember this time as the first time I ever learned how to do two things really well, put up an emotional wall to protect myself and reach for the nearest tangible vice, in this case cigarettes, to artificially make myself feel better.

In the months that followed I began to struggle some in school. I was sick of trying to fit in and the emotional walls I was putting up were doing a pretty good job of alienating the friends I had anyway. I was starting to struggle more and more with some questions I had been having about myself and my sexuality but I was terrified of the answer and so I threw myself into a relationship with a girl that was very different from others I had dated. She was incredibly supportive of me just being me. She didn't care that I wasn't like the other boys at school and in fact seemed to like that I was more sensitive. I began writing a lot more during this time and she was always very encouraging of my writing.

She was older than I was and had therefore gotten her driver's license already. It was not long after Marcy's accident that I found myself asking my parents if I could go with my girlfriend out to lunch and shopping, she'd be driving. I can certainly understand their hesitation to let me go, but they did. Less than 20 minutes later they would get a call from a police officer letting them know we'd been in an accident. We hit a guardrail on highway 178, known to the locals as the river road. The car was smashed up pretty badly. We were ok, but shook up for sure. I don't recall exactly what happened really. I remember my girlfriend going off the road slightly on the right shoulder and into the gravel then the next thing I knew we were basically sideways and met the guardrail to the left in a head on collision. Looking back I can only imagine what that call must have been like for my parents, so close on the heels of the loss of their oldest to a car accident.

I didn't learn until later that we were the first to "test" the guardrails. Apparently they'd been put up along this winding road next to the river only months prior after urging by local residents that the road was not safe without them. My parents wrote a letter to the editor in the local paper shortly thereafter thanking the city for the guardrails and asserting that it very likely saved my life.

The thing I remember most about that time was that it was very confusing and hard to navigate. I liked this girl I was with but not the way I knew I was supposed to. I was not equipped to handle the loss of my sister and found myself often feeling depressed and alone, even when surrounded by people. I began to wish that there was a way that I could talk to Marcy and hear her respond. I wanted so badly to know she was ok, wherever she was. In my heart I always thought I believed in the after life, but it's way easier to believe in it when you don't have to wonder if anyone you love dearly is there or not. At this point in life I was pretty inexperienced with losing someone close. Josh's grandma dying was only a few months prior to this and it was very hard, but now it was even closer to home with the loss of Marcy and I hadn't completely figured out how to deal with the first loss yet. I remember wanting so badly to be able to talk to her and know where she was. There were a lot of hard days then, and I remember them all too well.

Chapter 13

Double Vision

One night, around Christmas time, our family was headed to dinner at a restaurant a couple of towns over. It was a caravan of cars since Jenny was riding with her boyfriend Keven with an "E", Katie with her husband Kevin with an "I" (we don't actually call them that but I have always kind of wanted to), and I think it was just Bobbi and I in the backseat of Mom and Dad's car. I can't remember which car Nick was riding in or if he was driving himself. I know he wasn't married yet and I don't recall him dating anyone around this time. I digress.

I was particularly sad this evening and missing Marcy more than ever. It was getting close to Christmas time and I wasn't loving the idea of a Christmas without her there. I was looking up at the clouds in the night sky out the window of the backseat of my parents big old chevy caprice (old school looking cop car).

As I looked up I saw my sister Marcy appear in the clouds. She had this bright light around her and she was smiling in a way I have never seen before. The most perfect, contented, happiest smile I have ever seen. It took me a second to realize past her smile that she was holding babies in her arms, two brand new little bundles, one in each arm. I remember thinking I should point this out to the others in the car but I was mesmerized. Just as I was about to tell Bobbi to look I heard Marcy's voice like a soft whisper in my ear. I was looking at her in the clouds and yet hearing her as though she was sitting right next to me in the car whispering in my ear, it was so strange and so wonderful at the same time. She said, "two, there's going to be two". She was so happy and I had this overwhelming feeling she was somewhere amazing.

When we got to the restaurant I was so struck by the experience that I couldn't eat. Everyone else ordered and I said I wasn't hungry. Mom was worried by this but since I'd been kind of moody and brooding as of late I think she chose to not pick this particular battle with me that night. My sister Katie has always been kind of the protector type and I guess she noticed me staring off a little too much so she took me aside and into the lobby area of the restaurant and asked me what was going on. I made her swear not to tell anyone for fear everyone would think I was crazy, but I told her what I saw, in detail. She hugged me, promised me she wouldn't say anything and we rejoined the rest of the group at the table.

I think it was only a few months later that Katie found out she was expecting her first child. I remember hearing the news and immediately getting a lump in my throat. It was twins, I knew it was twins, Marcy told me it was twins. I kept my mouth shut though and didn't say anything. A short while after finding out she was pregnant she had her first ultrasound. I will never ever for the rest of my life forget what it felt like in that moment when I saw the two little peanuts on the ultrasound picture instead of one. I cried for happiness of these new little babies that would be coming into our life and I cried from pure joy that it was true, what I saw was real and my sister Marcy was indeed in a better place.

They say to have faith is to believe in that which you cannot see. My mother taught me that and I remember thinking, well wouldn't it be a whole lot easier if you could just see it. I understand faith so much more than I did when I was younger but I will be forever grateful that God knew I needed to see to believe in that moment in my life. I think he knew that I would never be able to get past Marcy's death and move on without something more tangible to hold onto. He gave me an incredible gift by letting me see Marcy holding my nieces Abigail and Emily (now in their 20's and starting their own business together) before they were even born. Two of the greatest moments of my life include seeing them in Marcy's arms that night, then holding them in my own barely a year later.

It was around this same time that I was finally able to start accepting Marcy's death. I've never truly gotten over it, but finding a way to accept it and soldier on was so important. I'd been writing a lot of poetry in those days and most of it was pretty heavy and filled

with sadness but the one I am sharing with you now
was the first to include any kind of acceptance or
peace. I remember I'd gone to the cemetery to talk to
Marcy one day and that's when I wrote the following:

There's a shadow of a doubt
Beneath the shadow of a tree
Still I am not certain
For with my eyes, I did not see

I kneel in the grass
Why, I am not sure
I try to hear her voice
Is it the wind or is it her?

Here within the shadow
Lies an emerald stone
Blanketed with leaves
Of a past wind blown

I remember years ago
The piles of leaves we'd rake
Are you hiding in there now
Waiting for my hand to take

I brush the leaves aside
An answer to my prayer
A stone with just her name
Her soul – it is not there

Here beneath this shadow

Lies nothing but the need
Of a place to go and cry
A place to go and grieve

Still there is no answer
Where then can she be
If she's not beneath this tree
And not at home with me

Came a whisper from the air
In your heart, I'll always be
In the winds and in the rains
In the shadows of the trees...

Chapter 14

It's Time

Marcy had been gone less than a year. I was struggling to figure out how to make myself feel more than just friendship toward my girlfriend. Katie was getting more and more pregnant with the twins by the day and Jenny and her boyfriend Keven were hitting it off unlike I had seen with any past relationships she'd had. I really liked this one, he was funny and kind and wasn't mean to me like some of the others. I remember hoping she'd keep him around.

Mom and Dad were doing their best to cope but I honestly don't know what it was like behind closed doors for them at this time. I remember hearing both of them gently crying when they thought no one was around on more than one occasion in those days.

This next part I am sharing is hard for me as putting down on paper here will be the very first time it's been anywhere other than in my head. I have never shared this particular bit of my truth with anyone. Around this time, full on horrible puberty for me, which by the way if you are reading this and you have a child going through puberty, please try to remember how awful it is, what a confusing time for every person to have to go through.

As I was saying around this time was when I started having dreams about my future. I remember one recurring one in which I was a grown up, in a suit and tie, heading to work and as I turned to say goodbye to my wife before I left the house, there was a man, my spouse was a man. He was attractive and had kind eyes and a big smile and he would wish me a good day at work and I would walk out the house feeling both confused and extremely comfortable at the same time. It was like this dream kept giving me a glimpse into a future that I didn't understand but also really wanted. The secret isn't the dream though, the part I have never shared is that I was so concerned by it that every time I would wake up from the dream I used to say to myself "it's time". "It's time" was my way of telling myself to stop putting off ending my life and just do it already.

At this time, then President Clinton, a democrat and certainly labeled a liberal, had passed DOMA (the defense of marriage act) recognizing marriage as between a man and a woman. Knowing that even the so called liberal party was anti-gay marriage was very telling of the way the nation felt about it. Ellen had come out on her sitcom and lost everything including the show as a result. Stock gay characters were not prevalent on tv and in the small town I lived in I didn't know anyone who was gay. The few things I had heard about gay people were only bad and included spending eternity in hell after you die. My addled little 15 year old brain had decided that if I ended my life on my terms before anyone ever found out about it, that I could escape the eternal damnation of being gay. At that time I couldn't even say I was gay in my own head much less out loud. The recurring dream was obviously not the only issue. As I said, I was going through puberty. The same way I assume the other boys in my class were starting to notice the girls in a different way, I was having the opposite experience. It was so confusing because I struggled so hard to make friends with other boys and got along great with girls. I remember thinking how easy it would have been to suddenly be attracted to girls because I could talk to them without issue, way easier than I could talk to the boys. The sudden attraction to the boys was so frustrating to me at the time.

After what seemed like an eternity of the recurring dream where I got a glimpse of a future with a husband, I woke from it one night, said to myself "it's time" and went to the medicine cabinet and took a bunch of pills. I think it was either Tylenol or ibuprofen, I don't recall, but I took a lot of them. I went back to my room, laid back down in my bed and within 10 minutes I started to panic. I realized I didn't really want to die and now I didn't know what to do. I also had no idea if what I had just taken would actually kill me or just make me really sick. As I had done many times in life prior to this point and many times in my life since, I turned to my sister Bobbi. I went into her room and told her what I did. She did the right thing by waking my parents right away. I don't remember much about the ride to the emergency room but I remember being told that my dad carried me in his arms to the front doors and banged on the doors when they wouldn't open. One of my sisters told me later in life that my mom said seeing Dad carrying me and demanding urgent help was powerful for her; I guess it helped re-affirm for her that her husband would do anything for his kids and how much love he had for them.

I remember the awful black chalky stuff they made me drink in the emergency room and how terrible I felt when a very pregnant Katie showed up in tears. I felt so selfish and awful for putting my family through that, and for what? Because I was too scared to face who I really was? I knew I had to tell them the truth, but I just couldn't do it yet. I remember everyone wanting answers as to why I did it and I just kept telling everyone I was depressed over the loss of my sister. It wasn't untrue, I was depressed by the loss of Marcy and nothing felt the same anymore, but at that time I couldn't bring myself to tell anyone the real reason.

I think it was almost a year later when I decided I didn't want to keep my secret anymore. I woke up one morning, 16 years old, tired of feeling like I was 2 different people, and said out loud to myself, I'm gay. What followed were conversations, increasing in their difficulty, with my family members. I told Bobbi first. I think I told Jenny second and Mom third. I remember driving to Katie's house to tell her and asking Mom to tell Dad while I was gone. I regret having waited so long to tell my brother. I wasn't very close with him then like I am today and I was so scared how he'd react. I don't remember when I told him but I know it was a long time after everyone else.

When I arrived home from telling Katie, Mom and Dad were sitting in the dark in the living room. I sat down and no one said anything. I finally broke the silence and said, "Dad, please say something, anything, just please say anything". He turned to me and said "you're my son, I love you, and that's all that matters to me."

Chapter 15

Twilight Zone

There were about 2 years between my coming out to my family and the first time I ever met another gay person. I can't begin to describe how lonely those years were for me. I made the most of my final years of high school though, choosing to come out to only a very small handful of people beyond my family. I confided in my dear friend Virginia, we called her Vinnie for short. She and I had been friends since kindergarten, having grown up together through all the same teachers, classes, and small-town happenings.

Our Junior and Senior years of high school Vinnie and I became even closer friends than we had been in our younger years. Confiding in her was incredibly important to me as it was my first timid attempt at trying to figure out who I was and how the world was going to perceive me now. Vinnie and I had so many wonderful moments of laughter and friendship in those years, we even had our senior pictures taken together. Her friendship was and remains so important to me, but I still remember feeling so out of place during this time.

How do I begin to describe what it feels like to be the queer fish in the straight pond? When you're young, fitting in often seems like the most important thing ever. When someone points out the ways in which you are different from everyone else, it can feel like the end of the world. Here I was, finally being honest with myself and the important people in my life, and what did it matter? I don't know what I thought would happen when I came out. I guess I thought that finally being honest about who I was would somehow change just how alone I felt in the world. The truth is, for a time, it actually made me feel even more alone. The entire scope of my world consisted of boys and men that were very much the same. They loved hunting, fishing, driving some sort of device on wheels through some sort of pile of mud. Don't get me wrong, I didn't and still don't take issue with any of these interests, they're simply not mine. What I did take issue with and still do today, is the male ego, machismo, whatever you want to call it. Nothing bothers me more than condescension and egotistical behavior. Where were the sensitive boys that loved to bake, write poetry, and perform in school plays?

Imagine yourself and all your interests, whatever they may be, being plopped down in the middle of some sort of twilight zone episode wherein everything that matters to you is seen as strange to everyone else around you. Imagine trying to enjoy any parts of your life when everything you actually like to do brings about ridicule. Imagine pretending to like all sorts of things you couldn't care less about just to bring about a much needed sense of relief, however brief, from the constant microscope of judgement placed on all your actual interests. It's lonely. It's hard to write about it because I have no desire to relive it. But I submit to you that it's not forever. If you are reading this and identify with these feelings, please know, it can get so much better. I won't pretend it's easy, but it is possible. You can get out, expand your horizons, grow and experience the world.

I remember during those years between 16 and 18 that there were many times where I felt like I was doomed to a life of solitude. Friends like Vinnie certainly helped me through those years but feeling like there was nobody else like me out there in the world was very hard. The irony looking back is that I am sure there were others like me, even in my small town, but I didn't know it, maybe they didn't either. Part of the reason I talk a lot about the importance of traveling, seeing other places, understanding other cultures, is because of these two years of my life. Even as I lamented many days about feeling alone, I always knew in my heart that I would venture beyond the imaginary borders of my small town someday, and someday I would finally get to meet someone like me.

Chapter 16

Jessie's Girl

A couple of months before I graduated high school, I turned 18 and moved into my own little apartment. I remember thinking how cool it was to live on my own and go to bed when I want and have friends over anytime I want. I also had to work a full time job while finishing up high school, that part was less fun.

As much fun as it was being out in the world for the first time, I hadn't strayed more than about 20 miles from my home town. I enjoyed living on my own initially but the little town I was in lacked any more diversity than the little town I left. The most exciting thing about that town, Cadott, WI, was that it was exactly halfway between the equator and the north pole. Well that, and the fact that it was home to the famous country fest and rock fest grounds every summer, but I was young and broke and could never afford the tickets back then.

I reiterate, it is so very lonely when you feel like you're the only person like you in the whole world. Eventually I would grow tired of living in a small town by myself. As a country, we had just been through 9/11, a terrorist attack that killed thousands of US citizens.

Planes had been hijacked and flown into the twin towers of the world trade center in New York and the Pentagon was also hit. I remember I had been home at Mom and Dad's when it happened and watching in terror on their TV as the 2nd tower was hit. I had many emotions about 9/11 and anyone who is old enough to remember it will be able to tell you where they were and what they were doing when they first heard the news. For me, 9/11 gave me a sense that no where was truly safer than anywhere else and that tomorrow was not promised to any of us. Indirectly, it is what gave me the desire to live each day with more purpose and take more chances. Life was fragile I had learned when losing Marcy and 9/11 all the more solidified my "live for today" mentality.

My sister Bobbi and the boy next door, Josh were newly-weds at this time and they had moved to Stevens Point, a bigger city a couple hours away from our hometown. They were just starting out and had no kids yet at this time and I moved into their spare bedroom, got a job at the same place my sister was working and shared in my portion of the rent and utility costs.

While living in Stevens Point, I was able to find a group of people at the local college that met every week that called themselves the GSA (gay straight alliance). I will never forget walking into that room the first time. I don't think I've ever been so nervous in my life. The idea that there were other people like me and I was going to finally meet some of them was almost too overwhelming. I remember seeing some young men my age, very cute, smile and wave at me but I was so painfully shy when it came to this particular part of my life and this was all so new. I was and always had been more comfortable around women. I settled into a seat next to a very chatty and kind young woman.

At this time, it was unfortunately not terribly uncommon for parents of gay children to disown them and throw them out of their house. The young woman I sat next to was going through exactly that. I was never more grateful for the parents and family I was blessed with than I was in that moment listening to her story. I was surprised to learn that one of her biggest challenges was affording college. Her parents were quite well off but had refused to continue to pay her college tuition when she told them she was gay. She was a very upbeat and confident person despite her situation and very matter of factly explained that she was happy to get student loans and do this herself, but she couldn't because her parent's income was too high.

She would go on to explain that she needed to be emancipated from her parents if she had any hopes of getting student loans and staying in school. That's when she told me she had arranged to marry her best friend, Jessie, a gay man who was happy to help her out in this endeavor and who had similar family dynamics to her. I don't recall if she introduced me to Jessie that same night or if it was the next week, but it was definitely a short time between meeting her and meeting him.

Jessie would become my first ever boyfriend and the complicated relationship and living situation between him and his friend/wife, the first gay person I ever met (to my knowledge) would prove to be too difficult to navigate. Lots of lessons learned on that one, but finally I had experienced what it was like to date someone I am attracted to. What an incredible feeling it was to feel like myself for the first time in my life.

I lost touch with both of them quite a few years back, but I think of them both from time to time and hope they are doing well. I hope they both found everything they ever wanted in life. I also hope that they were able to find a way to have good relationships with their families. Family has been so important to me in my life, I always hated that they didn't have the same.

Chapter 17

Lessons in Love

After Jessie I learned that dating in the gay world didn't have to be so different from straight dating. I learned that it was ok to have expectations and that I didn't have to completely fall into someone else's world to date them. To clarify, there was nothing wrong with Jessie's world, it just wasn't what I wanted. The following year, Bobbi and Josh were expecting their first child and their 2nd bedroom that I was living in was going to be needed for a nursery. I had moved on as I said from Jessie and I was dating a charming young man and it was going well. We decided, probably a little too hastily, to move in together. For a while it was bliss. I remember thinking for the first time that my life could be just like my siblings lives. I could have a partner, a place of our own, live life basically the same way they did.

We had lots of friends and both enjoyed decorating our apartment and hosting people for drinks, or movie night, or board games. I remember one year we drove to the BGC (Big Gay conference) together with a caravan of friends all the way to Columbus, Ohio. It was a fun event and the first time I had ever been around so many people just like me all at once. I even got to meet Ru Paul in the hallway leaving the conference, he's even taller in person than he is on TV!

On the way back from the conference our car broke down somewhere in Ohio near the Indiana state border. We eventually had to settle into a little motel and send our friends on without us. Our car was fixed the next morning and delivered to us from Fudge's autobody by Fudge himself. A large flannel clad man with a thick accent that suggested he was a transplant from a southern state. Keys in hand, we bid farewell to Fudge and we were back on the road. I remember we stopped and bought a fish for our fish tank and named it after the town we'd been briefly stranded in, though the name escapes me now. Why we didn't name the fish fudge I am not sure, seems like a missed opportunity.

Life was pretty good, but I couldn't help feeling like I was playing house. I wanted so badly for my life to be just like everyone else's that I would try very hard to make things as "normal" as I could. This put a strain on our young relationship and I remember asking way too many questions about the future all the time. He put up with it like a champ but it was eventually me that realized that while we liked each other a lot, neither of us was right for the other for the long haul.

I would eventually strike out on my own for the 2nd time, this time more equipped to handle it and in a bigger city where I'd made a lot of friends.

I laugh looking back now at just how big I thought that city was, but for my frame of reference at the time and coming from the gravel roads of Mudbrook, this city might as well have been Chicago for how different it seemed to me. I recall the very first time I ventured out at night getting pulled over rather quickly. The cop approached my car window and explained that I was driving without my headlights on. It never even occurred to me to turn them on because the streetlights were so bright and prevalent. Where I grew up, if you didn't have your headlights on at night you wouldn't have made it 10 feet.

I had moved on from the job where my sister worked and was doing well and moving my way up at the insurance company in town. I had been promoted to supervisor and was making a little more money and feeling pretty confident. I made a lot of good friends and memories in Stevens Point.

After a year of living in my own cute little townhouse, going out with friends and co-workers most nights, and enjoying being close to Bobbi and Josh and their new little bundle, I eventually started to feel like something was missing. A lot of my friends were graduating college and taking jobs in other cities and states. I had thought about going to college myself but had still never landed on what field of study I would even pursue.

My lease at the townhouse was about to be up and I had to decide if I wanted to sign for another year. The choice I made next would set the stage and end up being the thing I referred back to with every adventurous decision I would make in the future. For the rest of my life, before any major decision I would remind myself of the chance I took at this point in life and use it as my reassuring courage that I had it in me to do it again, and again, and again.

Chapter 18

Southern Exposure

I was 21 years old, living and working in a city I had come to love. I had a lot of friends and a job at which I was excelling. There was something about signing my name on the dotted line of another year lease that made me pause and ask myself if maybe I didn't want something more, something else, something different.

A dear friend of mine, Martha, had recently moved from the city I was in, where we met, and she and her boyfriend and their son settled in southern Florida. They had gotten married and she was pregnant with kid number 2. I remember the day I was talking to her on the phone lamenting over whether I wanted to spend another year in the same place. She offered up her spare bedroom at her house in Florida and I remember laughing, thinking "I can't move there". But later that night I remember sitting in my little townhouse and thinking, "Why can't I move there?"

The rest happened very fast. I called Martha the next day, discussed details and told her I was just going to do it, I was in, head first, not overthinking it too much. I put in my two week notice at my work, told my landlord I wouldn't be renewing for another year, sold everything I owned that wouldn't fit in my hatchback, and before I knew it, I was on the road, headed south to sunny Florida. I had no job lined up but I had a little money in my pocket that I had saved up and knew I would have some time to figure it out.

My sister Katie made the road trip down with me and booked a one way flight home. I was so thankful for a car companion. I remember we listened to "The Funny Thing Is" Book on tape by Ellen DeGeneres and laughed until we had tears in our eyes for much of the drive. I also remember my driver's side window was stuck in the up position so the tollways were super interesting!

There was torrential rain as we drove through downtown Atlanta in the wee hours of the night and I believe that was about the time that Katie had to pee so bad we ended up pulling over in a Wendy's parking lot and she had to go behind a bush by the dumpsters. (if you read this part it means Katie said it was ok for me to keep it in the book).

We pulled into the parking lot of the apartment complex in Plantation, FL just outside Fort Lauderdale on a 100 degree day, exhausted and ready for a nap. Martha's husband Bo greeted us warmly and after very brief chatting, we both gladly accepted his offer to lie down in the other room and rest. I remember when I woke up, greeted by Martha, home from work and such a nice hug and so much excitement to see her again. I also remember heading out to my hatchback to start unloading some things. I had put all of my bedding into the original see through thick plastic zippable bed in bag thing it came in and it was on top of everything else in the back. When I opened the hatchback, the plastic of the bag had gotten so hot it melted to the rear window of my car and went right up with the hatch as I opened it, stuck right to the glass. I had to peel it off, taking half the window tint with it.

I was so excited for this adventure and I so adored Marth and her husband Bo. I found a job in less than a week, paying more than my old job. It seemed I was on track for a new life in a new climate with who knows what adventures to lie ahead.

I was so naïve. I was so young. I thought for sure this big change up was what I wanted. I thought I knew what it meant to be homesick because I had experienced it when I moved 2 hours from home, but usually when I got home sick I would drive the 2 hours home to see my parents. Now, here, in this place that felt like an entirely different world, homesick took on a whole new meaning. I didn't have the means with which to fly home anytime I wanted, nor the cash or time required to drive all that way. I didn't mind the new job and I loved spending time with Martha and Bo and their two little ones, but I missed home, a LOT. I didn't make it very long before I decided to go back. Martha was disappointed but she understood, I just bit off more than I could chew... and for my age, it wasn't so surprising really.

I didn't consider Florida a failure then and I don't consider it one today. As I mentioned previously, it's still the one thing I ever did against which I have measured all other things. I remind myself that when I was just 21 years old, I sold everything I owned, quit my job, moved across the country, and found a job in less than a week! It wasn't the right place for me at that time but it was the right mindset to give me the confidence that I could do literally anything, try anything, go anywhere. If it didn't work out, I would try something different, go somewhere different. The world was at my fingertips and suddenly anything felt possible.

Chapter 19

My *Roaring* 20's

Back from Florida but not 100% sure what I wanted to do next, I landed on my parents doorstep again. A reality that had happened for me at least a few times in my life. I think someone once called that a "boomerang kid", a kid that moves out on their own and ends up moving back in then ventures out again and so on. While the term is a little offensive to the boomerang himself, it wasn't wrong. I am beyond thankful that my parents were always there for me anytime I ever needed them, it's a big part of what gave me the confidence and success I enjoy today.

My early to mid-20's are a bit of a blur. I was back in my neck of the woods, of legal drinking age now, and surrounded by a LOT of friends that liked to go out drinking. I don't remember how long I stayed with Mom and Dad but it wasn't long. I would eventually end up moving in with my friend Adam in his little apartment near campus where he was going to school in Menomonie, WI.

The sheer volume of stupid stuff we did back then. We went out to the bars almost every night. I was in tech college in Eau Claire, the next town over, going for counseling. Adam was in school for HRT and we were both working the same 2nd shift schedule at the power company at night as customer service reps.

There were no gay bars where we lived and one small gay bar the next town over. I can't count the number of nights we spent there. I have lifelong friends I met there and I have one night stands whose names I can't remember that I met there. While the heavy drinking and the jumping from one relationship to the next of my 20's was not the healthiest life, I believe it was a time and a collection of experiences that I needed to learn from. And though heading out to the bar was the most common thing we did back then, it wasn't the only thing.

One year, Adam and I and a couple friends of ours went on a canoeing trip down the Brule river in the far northern reaches of WI, near the Canadian border. I will never forget sitting in my canoe with our friend munchkin after a mild rapids we had just maneuvered and wondering where the hell Adam and Nicole were, they'd been right behind us. A short while later a small bag of chips and a flip flop floated past our canoe. It was then then I looked up to see Adam and Nicole coming down the end of the rapids, canoe upside down, clinging to bottom of the overturned canoe and laughing hysterically.

There was the time we visited the cabin of a friend of ours and about 20 other people were there. Our friend had this cabin in the Northwoods and all kinds of fun ATV's and such. We sat around the campfire for hours and when it was time to head up to the cabin all the ATV's had already been taken by others who left the campfire before us. It was a long muddy trail from the firepit to the cabin and after losing both our flip flops to very deep mud while trying to walk it, we decided to take Adam's car up the trail since there were no 4 wheelers left. Adam was skeptical of this plan but I was much more comfortable with it since it was his car and not mine. I offered to drive and assured him it would be fine. I don't believe we made it more than 50 feet before a giant soft mud hole on the left side of the trail opened up and swallowed half of Adam's car, causing the passenger side door to face straight up to the sky. We climbed out of the unobstructed side and made our way to the cabin where our friend was thrilled to have an excuse to use his new tractor to pull us out. Adam still brings that story up to this day when he wants to make me feel guilty. In my defense, I did pay for a car wash the next day... it didn't help, but it's the thought that counts.

There was the time we went to Las Vegas and Adam forgot his contact lens holder. He decided to use a water glass in the hotel bathroom to keep them in at night. He failed to mention this to me however and I may or may not have drank his contact lens in the middle of the night when I got up for a drink of water.

For every dumb thing I did to him there are another 20 stories of things he did to me but regardless of how silly a lot of it was or how looking back some of it was probably dangerous… we survived it and built a best friendship in our 20s that we still have today.

Eventually I would change my field of study from counseling to culinary arts and we would settle into enjoying more evenings in, playing board games and watching movies with a nice glass of wine instead of being out in a crowded bar. We both did our fair share of dating during this time and we would provide each other advice and borrow clothes for dates. It was a fun time and I wouldn't trade it for the world.

During this same time there was a bit of a baby boom happening in my family. All the siblings were now married at this point and my list of nieces and nephews was growing bigger and bigger. Jenny married that guy I said I hoped would stick around, Keven with an "E" and they were well on their way to kid number 2 of their eventual 3. Katie and her Kevin with an "I" now had the twin girls and a son. Nick and his wife had a daughter and a son now and Bobbi and Josh were somewhere in the process of their eventual 6 total kids. TJ had remarried a nice girl named Jess after my sister Marcy passed away and they had a son together, Trent, giving Miki and Jake a new little brother to love.

It seems strange to sum up so many amazing moments in one little paragraph here, but as I stated up front, it doesn't feel right to try to describe all my siblings life moments for them. What I can tell you is that it was rare for me to miss any of them. I was in the waiting room pacing back and forth for the birth of nearly every child. I remember the look on my brother's face when he came into the waiting room, a Dad for the first time, to tell us his daughter had been born and a couple of years later when his son was born. I remember the same look on the faces of my brother in laws with each of their kids when they too would enter the waiting room to tell us, "he's here!" or "she's here". I adore being an uncle and I love all my nieces and nephews so much. Anyone that knew me during the timeframes when so many of them were being born will tell you it wasn't at all uncommon for Joe to take an impromptu day off work and be on his way somewhere across the state to meet his newest niece or nephew.

It was at this time in my life that I was getting that feeling again. That, "I want something more feeling". I had been loving my 20s and the fun and the going out and the dating countless people, but I wanted something more. Adam had met someone and moved out of state and I was now living on my own again in a little apartment in Eau Claire, WI.

I started looking for more serious relationships and dated a couple of guys, one for an entire year even, but I realized that wanting a serious relationship is not a good reason to be in one. Not wanting to live alone was another really bad reason to be in a relationship. I eventually moved in with my good friend Sarah and threw myself into my work. I was working in the insurance industry again and really started focusing on being successful with the company I was with. I eventually got promoted to a supervisory position and

I knew if I kept at it I would go even further with this company. I was making a name for myself there and for the first time in my life I felt content, like I didn't need anyone else in my life. I was 26 years old, I was doing well, I enjoyed my friends and my work and I decided to stop looking for Mr. Right, I didn't need him.

Chapter 20

Boy Meets World

December 23, 2009. Adam was home visiting friends and family for the holidays. He and I were in my apartment with other friends, listening to music, catching up, having a couple of drinks, and getting ready to call a cab to take us to our old favorite drinking spot from our early 20s. Adam's phone rang. It was an old friend and co-worker of his from one of the hotels he had worked at in town before he moved out of state. She had planned to meet up with us that night and he thought maybe she was calling to say she was running late. It turns out she was calling to say that she had a new co-worker at the hotel, he was gay, from out of town, just moved here, didn't know anyone, and she wanted to invite him to join us for the evening.

Adam looked to me, gave me the quick overview and I gave him a prompt thumbs down. This was my only night to hang out with my best friend who had moved far away and we had only a handful of visits per year now. He gently provided a no go to his friend on the phone and I could hear her continuing to protest so I eventually sighed and gave him the thumbs up.

Another hour or so went by, drinking and adding songs to our playlist at my apartment, Adam's friend showed up and we were just waiting on her co-worker to join us and then would all be headed out on the town. At one point the song "If I could turn back time" by Cher came up in the playlist. I realize this is a gay stereotype, but I don't care, I adore that song. I cranked it up loud and we all sang along laughing.

Shortly into the song there was a knock on my front door. I opened the door and there stood a handsome young man in his mid-20's looking an awful lot like a cross between Corey from the show Boy Meets World and an early 2000's Justin Timberlake. His name was Jamie Rady and if you read the back cover of this book, the special thanks preceding the first chapter, or noticed my last name is also Rady, then it should come as no surprise to you that this is the man that would eventually become my husband.

He'll tell you looking back that he knew I was hitting on him later that night when I complimented the cologne he was wearing. He says he knew it was a line because he had forgotten to put on cologne and even considered turning back to go get it but decided against it since he was already running late, an issue of his that persists, I promise you, to this day.

He will also tell you how close we were to never having met at all that night. The apartment complex I was living in at the time had several main entrances. It was confusing and there was no signage. It was almost impossible to order food for delivery and ever have the driver actually find the right apartment. He had arrived well before I cranked the Cher song that night and was close to giving up having not found a way into the building that led to any door with my apartment number. That's when he heard the song by Cher playing and decided that perhaps he should follow the music. Again, a stereotype but one for which I am thankful, obviously it worked out in my favor.

The next year was one of the best in my life to that point. Jamie and I began seeing each other nearly every day. He was living an hour north of Eau Claire so would often spend the night at my place during the work week so as not to have such a long commute to work every day.

He had met almost all my family and they all liked him as much as I did. I will never forget that my mom immediately said he looked like the Boy Meets World kid too! I was finding him to be charming, funny, kind, smart and at the same time I was irritated because I had literally just declared I wasn't looking anymore. He will also tell you that part of what attracted him to me was my lack of neediness and my desire to be my own person with my own interests and not just fall into his world. You'll remember my issues with that in past relationships from earlier. It's amazing looking back how I see the exact purpose of the relationships and situations I went through and how they were preparing me for the right one at the right time.

About 6 months into the relationship, we both fell in love. He said it first but I didn't hesitate. I had wanted to say it already at that point and it felt right. I met his family around this time and while I was very nervous, I ended up having a nice dinner with his parents and sister and getting to know them pretty well.

We started joining each other for family holiday get togethers and before we knew it, it was over a year later and we were talking about plans to live together when my lease was up in a few months.

One week after the first time we ever floated the idea of moving in together I got a call from the CEO of my company that would prove to be one of the first real tests of our relationship.

Jamie and I out for drinks with friends, early on in our dating.

Chapter 21

Discovering Columbus

In the spring of 2011, I was loving life a LOT. My job as a supervisor was going so well that they had given me my own client to manage. Client management was reserved for the National Account Coordinators and had never been entrusted to a supervisor before. Jamie and I were clicking right along and starting to talk about looking for a place together and life was good. That's when I got a call from a number I didn't recognize.

I was in a meeting with my boss at work when my cell phone started going off. Normally I'd just let it go to voicemail but it was sitting on the conference table and my boss glanced at it and recognized the number as the personal cell of the CEO of the company. I thought she was messing with me, I wasn't even sure he knew my name much less why he'd have my number. She hurried me out of the room and told me to answer it asap. It wasn't a joke, it was indeed the CEO and he was calling with a job offer. He told me he was expanding the company and would need to add another National Account Coordinator to the staff. He said he asked around and my name kept coming up. He said he heard how well I handled the onboarding of the client I was given and he offered me a big bump in pay to my first ever salaried position. I was speechless. I was so excited and thrilled for the opportunity and just as I was about to say yes to the offer, he stopped me and said, "you're going to need to talk to Jamie about it first.". Now I am really confused, not only does he know me and is offering me a job but he knows I am with Jamie. Not only does he know I am with Jamie but he wants me to talk it over with him first? Before I could respond that's when he said, "The job would mean having to move to Columbus, Ohio." It seems he wanted me to take this new role but also help start up the new office in Ohio.

I remember wringing my hands until they were sore while I waited for Jamie to arrive to my place that night. Here was this great guy that I am in love with and who I wasn't even looking for when he showed up at my door. This guy who loves me back and who not one week ago agreed we should talk about moving in together. How do I tell him about this opportunity? Where does he fit in the mix of all of it? On top of it all, I wasn't the only one with an amazing job opportunity. He had just accepted his first ever GM job at a hotel not long before all this. It was a big deal at his age to be a General Manager of a hotel already and on top of that, he was still in college, finishing up his degree in the hotel program at UW Stout.

Jamie arrived and I worked up my courage and told him about the opportunity and Ohio and all of it. In my heart of hearts I hoped against hope that he would say he would go with me, but I absolutely couldn't ask him to do that. As it turns out, I never had to ask. He calmly said we'd work it out and he would come with me to Ohio, though it might have to be a little later than when I move so he could finish school. To this day he still has that ability to approach just about anything with that same calm, rational, let's talk this through kind of tone. I both love him and am jealous of him for that. I suppose it's good that both of us aren't like me in that area though, I tend to idle at "oh no what are we going to do?!" so it's helpful to have him there to reign me in when needed.

My company graciously offered to pay moving costs for both of us and we flew out a couple weeks later to scout possible apartments. We found one we liked quickly and signed the lease. I moved a couple months later and Jamie followed a couple months after that when he finished up school. He found a different remote work job when he moved and the next year was all about learning how to live together and making new friends in a new state far from everything we'd known and gotten used to.

We were so thankful to have met Erin and Matt early on. A nice couple with whom we'd end up spending much if not most of our time that year. Erin and I worked together and hit it off and her boyfriend Matt and Jamie hit it off the first time we double dated and the rest is history. Bowling leagues, favorite restaurants, get togethers at each other's houses. We learned of Matt's passing last year. We were heartbroken to hear from Erin the details of Matt's health decline and passing at such a young age. Another life lesson. Learning how hard it is to stay in touch with people that are important to you. The year we left Ohio I was so certain we'd stay in close contact with Matt and Erin. Learning that some friends come in and out of your life for a particular season is something with which I honestly still struggle. I want everyone I've ever loved to live on the same street as I do and follow me wherever I go, is that so much to ask?

That year in Ohio was important for so many reasons and having Matt and Erin as our friends certainly made it a fun ride. Jamie and I were learning each other's living habits and adjusting to cohabitation. We were also traveling back to Wisconsin pretty regularly. My primary office was still back in central Wisconsin and there were times I had to meet a client there. Often times, I chose to drive rather than fly because Jamie could then go along. I recall one particular trip back to Wisconsin when we decided to stay at my old apartment rather than renting a hotel room. When we'd left Wisconsin, a friend of ours sublet my old place and often offered for us to stay there when we'd travel back.

One particular time I recall I had been running late to get to my old office. I was rushing from my old apartment down the very familiar road on which I had lived for a long time. As I sped through a particular stretch of Fairfax street I looked up in my rearview mirror to see blue and red flashing lights. I remember sitting there thinking how much later I was going to be to work and also how on earth am I going to talk my way out of this ticket. Before the cop approached my window it suddenly occurred to me that I was driving a rental car with Ohio license plates. The cop approached the window as I was still working out what I was going to say in my head. As you might expect, he explained how fast I was going in comparison to the posted speed limit. Thinking I was so very clever I quickly explained that I was from out of town, unfamiliar with the territory, and here only on business. That's when the cop asked to see my driver's license. I remember my heart sinking into my stomach as I reached for my wallet, remembering 10 seconds too late that my driver's license was still a Wisconsin license. Not only had I not bothered to get an Ohio driver's license yet, but the street address on my Wisconsin ID was Fairfax street. Yes, the very street where I was currently sitting alongside the road explaining my unfamiliarity with this strange new land as a native Ohioan.

I submit to you that the length of time that the cop spent back in his squad car with my license in hand before coming back to my driver's side window seemed like an absolute eternity to me. I could hear my mother's voice in my head reminding me this is exactly why it's never ok to lie. I was envisioning being arrested and having to call Jamie to come bail me out of jail. I was wearing a 3 piece suit and managed to sweat all the way through to the jacket.

Approximately one eternity later, the officer approached my window. He handed me my license and said he was going to issue me a warning and asked that I be more mindful of the posted speed limits. I believe I mustered a thank you and an of course officer and another thank you and started to reach for the button to roll my window back up. Before I could hit the button the officer said, "one more thing, I notice you have a Wisconsin ID... and I noticed your address is Fairfax street". I knew it, he was messing with me on the whole just a warning thing, I'm getting booked, I'm going to the big house. Literally in this moment the only response I could muster was "ya, ummm, about that, funny story...". Thank the good Lord in heaven that the cop cut me off mid-sentence because I have no idea how I was going to finish that sentence. He smirked and said "just slow down through here alright?". Just like that, he was on his way and I was in the clear. My suit on the other hand was no longer presentable for work.

Jamie and I were pretty lucky with as much driving we did between Wisconsin and Ohio back then to not have had any additional incidents with law enforcement. I recall the occasional letter in the mail now and then reminding us of a toll we'd forgotten to pay, but that was about it. I also recall obeying the speed limits much more regularly thereafter. Life was clicking along well and we were enjoying living together and getting to know the city.

Columbus, OH had and I assume still has a pretty substantial and nicely laid out gay district. We became very fond of several bars and restaurants, but one of our absolute favorites was a place called "Level". They had a chill relaxing dinner vibe to start the evening with high end delicious entrée's to choose from. Later in the evening tables would clear out and it was a completely different place, a dance club with excellent music and always busy.

We enjoyed hosting friends and family that made the long trip out to see us throughout our time there. I recall all my siblings and my Mom and Dad making the journey out to stay with us one time. We turned our living room and 2nd bedroom into air mattress equipped sleeping quarters to accommodate their weekend stay and they all went out to the gay district with us for dinner and drinks one night.

I remember feeling incredibly seen and loved during that visit. Prior to this it never even occurred to me that my parents and siblings would ever join me at a gay establishment. It was good for me to see their willingness and I think they'd tell you it was good for them to see that whatever they may have imagined, the places we went, the food we had, the people with whom we interacted, were not so very different from any other type of place. With the exception of the random clown that showed up at Level briefly causing my Mom to run outside until he left, it was a pretty great night. I still have no idea why someone was there dressed as a clown, I fear them just as much as my mother did so was happy to join her outside until he left. Never saw him there again after that.

Yes, Ohio was going well, living together was going well, and to me, it seemed like the perfect time to talk about getting a dog. What better way to make a new living situation, new state, new everything more manageable than a new puppy! If there was a sarcasm font, I'd have used it on that last sentence. I didn't care though, how unreasonable it was to throw yet another monkey wrench into the mix of our lives, I had never really had an indoor pet and I really had my heart set on getting a dog.

Chapter 22

Georgie

It was early September 2011. I'd been dropping enough hints about wanting a dog to Jamie that we were at the point where he was reluctantly going along with at least "looking". I'd seen an ad online from a woman whose mother had passed away. She had two Pomeranians when she died and the female was pregnant. She needed to find them all homes. She had several young kids and wasn't in a place to take care of one much less a whole family of dogs. By the time I saw the post all dogs had found homes except one. A precocious runt of the litter who refused to walk, choosing instead to gleefully prance everywhere he went. They hadn't named him officially though the kids were fighting over the names Tanner and Butterscotch, neither of which he seemed to respond to. Jamie agreed we could message the woman and inquire.

We met her in an Aldi parking lot in a not so great area of town outside of Columbus. We stepped out of the car and her side door on her van opened up and one of several small children hopped out and gently placed this tiny little fluff ball on the pavement. I knelt down and stuck out my hand and as the ad stated, he pranced all the way over to me. He crawled up into my lap, looked me in the eyes, and licked my nose, then settled back into my lap like he was finally home. I looked up at Jamie and if I remember right, his exact words were, "ahh crap".

That was it, we took him home and he was ours. We played around with lots of names and he just wasn't having it. At one point, I was on the floor with him, letting him decide which of the thousand toys we bought him he'd like to play with when I got the urge to pick him up and snuggle him again. He was very good about letting me hug him and even seemed to hug me back. I had a flashback of a Saturday morning cartoon I used to watch as a kid in which this large hairy monster thing picked up bugs bunny and snuggled him hard and said "Aww, I'm gonna love him, and hug him, and squeeze him, and name him George" (if you read that in the voice of the monster than you are at least as old as I am). As soon as I said George, his little head tilted sideways and he stared at me. I said it again and again he looked at me inquisitive. I looked at Jamie with a sort of "hmmm" and Jamie quickly got down on the floor and threw one of the toys down the hall, the puppy chasing after it, and then called out "come here George!" and for the first of what would be countless times thereafter, he came running back! It was settled, his name was George and to this day we're not sure if we picked it out or he did.

The next year consisted of all the usual puppy training and a dash of unusual. From the time he carefully opened the door on the DVD tower and gently removed one DVD and tore it to shreds. The DVD he chose was "the dog whisperer with Cesar Millan". Apparently he was trying to slow down our insistence on learning to train him.

There was the time Jamie made himself a breakfast sandwich and was about to sit down to enjoy it when the FedEx guy rang the doorbell. He set his plate down on the coffee table and answered the door, signed for the package, and turned around to see Georgie carefully removing just the sausage patty from between the two biscuits, leaving behind the egg and cheese then running at full speed down the hall with Jamie chasing after him.

The first time he discovered the ducks near the pond in front of our apartment and chased them into said pond and learned he doesn't like to get wet.

The countless times he tried to murder our fish. We had a large aquarium in our first apartment and a very large Oscar fish named Bubba. Georgie mostly never noticed him, the fish tank sitting up several feet off the ground and Georgie being all of a foot tall. But on occasion, when Bubba would swim to the front of the tank, Georgie would see him and start barking. He hated him so much. Now I don't know how this next part is possible, but on more than one, more than 5 even occasions, Georgie would wait until we were either gone or in another room and he would go to the outlet where the fish tank bubbler was plugged in and unplug it with his little teeth. We are convinced that he knew what he was doing as there were plenty of other outlets with varying other devices plugged into them and on no occasion did he ever attempt to unplug anything other than that one.

I am thankful that our Georgie is still with us today as I write this, laying at my feet fast asleep, none the wiser that I am telling his most embarrassing stories. He is 11 ½ years old now and while he requires some daily medications and a strict diet, he's overall happy and healthy and brings us an enormous amount of joy.

Chapter 23

Country Roads Take Me Home

About a year into our time in Ohio things were going well. I was doing well in my new role and enjoying it and I had helped to successfully get the new office up and running. Jamie was feeling less enthused about his remote work job and hoping to get back into something with hotels. He had a unique opportunity to possibly go into business with some friends in the industry but they were back in Wisconsin. We talked it over, I talked with my boss, who said the job he needed me to do in Ohio was wrapped, I'd done well, and if I wanted to continue in my new role from the original office back in Wisconsin he was fine with that. My role, after all, was to tend to clients across the entire country so my home base mattered a lot less once the new office was up and running and we had gotten all the proper personnel hired and in place.

The decision to move back happened pretty close to lease renewal time and left precious little time for apartment hunting back in Wisconsin. Ideally, we wanted to fly home and have some time to look and sign a lease somewhere but as it turned out, we'd end up spending a large chunk of time on a family vacation with Jamie's parents and sister during that month in which we should have been packing and apartment hunting. It was a wonderful trip to Las Vegas for a portion then on to Disneyland in California. I will never forget, nor will Jamie's family ever allow us to forget a particular morning of that trip. We were somewhere in between Vegas and Disneyland, having stopped at a hotel overnight on the drive from one to the next. We had a room right across the hall from Jamie's parents and his sister and her then husband were in a room next to theirs I believe.

Jamie and I had stepped out on our balcony early that morning to have a cigarette. It faced a wall of air conditioners and was covered on each side so there was no view in or out. Because of the lack of view we didn't bother to get dressed before we stepped out. Unfortunately for us, the sliding glass door locked behind us causing us to be trapped outside. Luckily, in addition to grabbing our cigarettes and lighters we had both also grabbed our cell phones before stepping out. After a call to the front desk and what seemed like a long wait but was probably less than 10 minutes, a very large maintenance man came crashing through the front door of our hotel room, located directly across from the glass sliding door to our balcony. I will never forget standing there on the other side of that glass, both of our hands carefully placed over sensitive areas and seeing both Jamie's Dad and sister in the hallway outside our hotel room watching and laughing so hard they had tears rolling down their cheeks. I certainly don't blame them, it was quite amusing.

With our family trip in which Jamie's family got to know a little more about me than I had anticipated now behind us, we realized there was really no time left to find a place back in Wisconsin in person. We had found a place that looked great online, just outside Eau Claire, in the country, in a small town called Elk Mound. Neither of us had never signed a lease on a place sight unseen. We took a leap of faith and signed electronically from Ohio.

I will never forget June 1, 2012, driving 10 plus hours with Georgie in the car toward a new home we'd never seen before. I remember praying as I got closer that it would at least be even somewhat close to how it looked online and if not that it would be at least habitable until we could find something else. Jamie wasn't with me that first day, I think he was in Madison and wouldn't be there until the next day. I stopped at the leasing office and picked up the keys and walked into our new home for the first time on the first day of our lease.

Luckily, it was beautiful, new carpet and fresh paint, well taken care of. Nice appliances, it even had a jacuzzi tub in one of the bathrooms! I remember it had in-floor radiant heat, something we have not had at any place we lived since and both miss.

The original job opportunity Jamie wanted to pursue when moving back was in the works but a little slow going. He ended up taking a job in the twin cities (St. Paul/Minneapolis, MN), his second General Manager position. It paid well but was a long commute every day. I was still traveling around the country from time to time for my job and while we were enjoying a newfound financial stability, we weren't getting as much quality time together as we had previously. We adjusted but both knew the long commute job for Jamie had a sell by date and at this point I had moved up as far as I could go with my company and was approaching the 5 year mark with them.

We had a lot of talk about "what's our next adventure" when living in our little place in the country. Also while living there, our relationship continued to grow stronger and our connection to each other became more and more significant. I remember Jamie had this habit of bringing me random pez dispensers at random times. Never for any occasion. The first time he ever gave me one he handed it to me and said, I saw this and thought it was cute, and it reminded me of you because you're also cute, and I thought it would make you smile. After that it sort of became a thing... every couple of months or so he'd randomly show up with a new pez dispenser he saw and picked up for me.

On December 23, 2012, 3 years to the day after we met, we were sitting at the dining room table in our little country home, wrapping Christmas presents together for our various family members. Jamie asked me to grab some more wrapping paper from the shelf in the bedroom and I got up to do so. I headed for the bedroom and when I opened the door what I saw would change my life.

Chapter 24

What is a Pezposal?

As the bedroom door swung open, I noted that it was odd that the door was closed in the first place as we usually left it open. I further noted that it was odd the light was off, since it usually stayed on all day until we went to bed. When I flipped on the light, in front of me were more Pez dispensers than I could count. They were set up on the bed, on the nightstand, everywhere in the room. I noticed the ones gathered on the night stand were in a more specific and seemingly purposeful design. I stepped closer and realized they were standing up in the shape of a heart. I looked closer and noticed that inside the heart, spelled out in pez candy were the words "Will You Marry Me?".

I remember this day so clearly and can't imagine I will ever forget it. I stood there, shocked, and still trying to take it all in. Finally it occurred to me what was happening and as I turned to head back out to the dining room, Jamie was right behind me, on one knee, ring in hand. I cried, I said yes, and it was one of the best decisions I ever made. I often think back fondly on my unique proposal or "pezposal" and remember how incredible I felt in that moment.

The next few months that followed our engagement consisted of more talk about what we wanted to do next. We talked wedding plans some but neither of us were in a huge hurry, knowing we'd want some time to plan just the right event. At this time, it wasn't legal for us to get married in the state of Wisconsin. The next state over, Minnesota, had legalized it and Wisconsin had agreed to recognize marriages from out of state but would still not allow the marriages to take place in Wisconsin. We talked about some ideas but it would be another year before we started really exploring our options for the big day.

I remember during this time both of us changing vehicles again. I had a habit (still do) of getting sick of whatever car I was driving within a year or two and wanting to trade it in for something different. I remember I bought the hamster car, a Kia Soul. You might remember the commercials for those when they first came out, the dancing hamsters were pretty popular. It was a funny perfect square of a boxy looking thing but I loved it. My habit of getting sick of my car was rubbing off on Jamie and during this time he ended up getting a new Toyota Camry. It was a nice car, bright red, but for some reason both of us will never understand, it had some sort of problem with attracting birds. The entire time we had that car I think Jamie reduced the overall general bird population by dangerous amounts. I swear I used to be terrified when he'd pull in our driveway each night of what kind of massacre was going to be in his front grill that day. There was even a day I recall when our neighbors were our front with their small children playing in the yard when Jamie drove in with a large bird once again stuck in his front grill. I remember standing in front of it awkwardly trying to block the carnage from the view of the small children while Jamie went to get the prying bar we kept on hand for this frequent issue. We used to joke back then as the birds attacking his car seemed to be increasing in size, that we didn't know what on earth we were going to tell the insurance company the day he eventually hits an ostrich. (spoiler alert, he never did)

In October of the following year, Jamie had had enough of the long, bird-destroying commute to the twin cities. I loved my job and the people I worked with, especially my friend Sandra, one of my first clients. An east coast girl with the attitude and accent to back it up. She and I formed a friendship that would endure well past our time working together. But I needed something more. It would be hard to even think about leaving this place. I had come up through the ranks at this company and worked my way up as high as I could go. Still both Jamie and I felt it was time to move on. We made a decision.

Chapter 25

Almost Madison

In mid-October of 2013, I was standing in my office at work, pulling books and paperwork from the shelves. Sorting through what needed to be shredded versus what needed to be labeled and archived for my replacement. Jamie and I had both given our notice at our respective jobs and decided we would be moving to Madison. Jamie to pursue starting his own business, and for me, I didn't quite know yet, but I had a couple of good leads. My sorting and shredding was interrupted when one of my co-workers stopped in and asked me to join an impromptu meeting in the conference room. Looking back I should have realized what was coming, but I honestly had no idea at the time. I will never forget walking into that room, filled with my friends and co-workers of the past almost 6 years. There were farewell balloons, good luck cards, a big cake, and 100 sets of eyes on me asking for a speech. I don't remember what I said in that moment, but I know I got choked up. This was, after all, the longest I had ever been with the same company and most of the faces I was staring at in that room were friends at this point, not just co-workers anymore. CarolAnn was one of those friends that I still see all these years later. Her friendship and guidance during my years at that job were so important to me.

That night we'd all go out to dinner and drinks. Lots of laughs and goofy pictures being taken. There were moments of sadness knowing at this point in my life the sad truth that I might very likely never see some of these people again. Many of them have remained a part of my life in some way, but I knew it would never again be like it was then, in that moment. We said our eventual goodbyes and the evening wrapped up with hugs and well wishes.

 A couple of weeks later, Jamie and I were on the road, headed for our new apartment in Madison. I remember we were both a little surprised at just how high the rent was in the area but had found a place we both liked. Jamie had taken a remote job again for some guaranteed income while he worked on his business and I had several interviews lined up for our first week in town. I ended up with a couple of offers and decided to take the one that I felt had better long term growth potential. It wasn't an easy decision since it meant starting out entry level until something opened up in the Client Management area. The pay was far less than what I had been making and there was no way of knowing how long it would be before I would have the opportunity to apply for a promotion.

Jamie's remote work job was less consistent than we hoped. There wasn't always enough work to keep him busy for a full work week. With the dramatic increase in our rent and the big reduction in both our income, money got tight very quickly. By month 3, we had exhausted our savings and were facing the facts that there was no way we could continue to afford Madison rental costs.

It was February of 2014, an ice storm had hit the Madison area hard the night before and the parking lot of our apartment complex was a virtual ice skating rink. Unfortunately, for us, it was also moving day. We'd negotiated our way out of our lease and our dear friend Rahne (pronounced rain) had offered up a small studio apartment in the basement of her and her Mother's home in a small but beautiful little town called Baraboo about an hour north of Madison. We both remember thinking originally at this time that our leap of faith didn't work out. We felt like we fell and we fell hard. We had nice incomes and a nice place in the country and we left it all behind and here we are 3 months later in the freezing cold, snow, and ice, moving half our things into a storage unit and the few things that would fit into a tiny studio apartment.

What we learned quickly in our time in that little apartment was that our leap of faith hadn't failed at all. As it turns out, that little studio apartment was exactly what we needed at the time. Looking back now, some of our best memories and biggest moments happened while living there. I also remember during this time being incredibly thankful for the life lessons of my childhood. If anybody knew how to pinch a penny or make a paycheck stretch, it was my parents. You'll remember the story of the watered down ketchup, the off brand cereal, and the watered down shampoo. There's something really amazing to me about the 20 20 vision of hindsight and the realization of the way that hard times of the past prepare you for hard times of the future. The plain truth is, I knew how to live on a tight budget. I knew how to make half a pound of ground beef into 3 pounds of delicious meatloaf. I was no stranger to clipping coupons, waiting for 2 for 1 sales, and taking advantage of any discount we could find.

During this time, I had a long commute to work every day, but the much more affordable living situation took a lot of stress off our shoulders. I kept working hard at my new entry level job and saying yes to every extracurricular project opportunity that came along. Jamie got a job with a hotel he'd helped open many years before and was back working with old friends and co-workers. We were happy and we were doing a lot of wedding planning from our little home-base.

6 months to the day into my new entry level job, I graciously accepted an offer for a huge promotion to a Client Manager position. My hard work had paid off. The position paid even more than my previous one in Eau Claire and the added bonus was the job would be entirely remote so no more long commute.

In June of 2014, a few weeks into the new job, I took 2 weeks off. Seems like odd timing being so new to the role but I had a very good reason.

Chapter 26

The Majestic Star

On June 27, 2014, aboard the beautiful Majestic Star, 4 story yacht, while floating down the St. Croix river, with over 100 of our closest friends and family on board with us, Jamie and I got married! It was the most perfect day. From our huge wedding party, to the Vera Wang tuxes, to the pez dispenser party favors, complete with explanations of how Jamie proposed.

We planned every detail and the day was a triumph. I remember as I was waiting to walk down the aisle toward Jamie with my mother standing next to me, she turned to me, squeezed my arm, and asked me if I was ready. I smiled and she smiled back and we headed down the aisle.

My dear friend Martha, who you may remember from the Southern Exposure chapter of my 21 year old misadventures trying to make a go of it in Florida, was a big part of our wedding day. Several months earlier while planning various details, Jamie and I got on the topic of who would actually perform the marriage ceremony. It didn't take me long at all to jump up and say, "Oh my gosh, I have the perfect person!".

I called Martha moments later and she didn't hesitate. By this time, she and Bo and the kids were living in Texas. Granting our request meant she'd have to get ordained officially first of all and second, fly her whole family to Stillwater Minnesota for our wedding weekend. As I said, though, she didn't hesitate. She was a wonderful officiant and even served as our "MC" for the wedding party introductions and the special dances later in the evening. Martha, a theater major and extremely confident and well-spoken young woman was the most perfect choice for this role. On top of which, I adored her then and now. Fun side note, Bo and Martha now have 3 children, the youngest of which was a happy little surprise conception the weekend of mine and Jamie's wedding.

Another fun fact; at Midwest weddings (though it may not just be the Midwest, I'm not sure) but it's very common place here for guests to clink their forks on their glasses during the meal while the married couple is seated with the wedding party at the head table.

This signals to the newly married couple that they must stop eating and give each other a passionate kiss so the guests can all cheer. Now imagine for a moment what that was like for Jamie and I staring out at a sea of faces in which we know for a fact that about half of them are very excited for us and not remotely averse to seeing two men kiss, while the other half is there because they love and support us but admittedly are less used to the idea and far less comfortable with it. While any couple married in an area where the glass clinking is common will tell you it's a little annoying, for Jamie and me it was almost comical because we knew there were definitely guests in attendance hoping they'd only have to see us kiss once during the ceremony! I am thankful for everyone that came to our wedding, and I don't hold against anyone that may have had a personal struggle with it but still showed up to support us.

I remember everything from our big day. The décor, the food, the dessert, the people laughing, dancing, and having a great time. The views of the water as we floated gently down the river. My niece, Miki, singing during the ceremony. As if inheriting her mother's beauty wasn't enough, she also inherited her beautiful singing voice. I remember dancing to *Cotton Eye Joe* with my former high school girlfriend turned life-long friend. She and I had danced to that song at our high school prom and it was an inimitable moment I will always remember. Jamie and I both knew we wanted our big day to be unique, and we got exactly that. Also, against all odds based on the semi open bar situation, not one person fell overboard... so that was a nice bonus.

We honeymooned in New Orleans the week following our wedding. We strolled through the farmers markets in the French Quarter. We ate beignets at the world famous Café Du Monde. And we had drinks at a different bar on Bourbon street every night. We rode the trolley that ran on tracks down Canal street, though our first attempt was a bit of an ordeal. Neither of us knew that there was an entrance door and an exit door and Jamie accidentally entered through the exit door the first time we tried to get on and it shut behind him too quickly for me to join. The trolley took off and headed down the tracks with Jamie on board and me standing on the sidelines watching his look of terror as he became a dot in the distance. Luckily for us, it makes frequent stops and we were reunited rather quickly. Aside from the trolley trouble, it was a week of absolute stress free relaxation and excitement for whatever new adventures would await us as a married couple.

Jamie trying a beignet at Café Du Monde in New Orleans. Can you tell he approved?

Chapter 27

Sunshine and *Rahne*

We were officially in the honeymoon stage after our wedding. We were still living in the basement apartment beneath our friend Rahne and her mom. I remember those days well. We didn't care that our bedroom and our living room had no wall to separate them. It didn't bother us that our kitchen was more of a small hallway with a 6 foot piece of countertop and a little fridge and tiny stove. We were young, newly married, and in love.

Rahne and her mother both lived in the house above us and the dynamic between all of us was kind of hilarious. Rahne's mom, Rosey was an interesting lady. I remember she used to like to go to the casino a lot back in those days. Rahne and Jamie would be off at work during the day. I would be working from home in the makeshift office I'd created with hanging sheets in the unfinished portion of the basement. Many days I remember Rosey appearing at the end of my workday in the opening of my hanging sheet office with drink in hand and asking me if I wanted to join her at the casino. I often joined her as I loved to play the cheap penny slots. Rosey was a somewhat boisterous woman, with a loud laugh and a lot of energy. She was endlessly doing projects in her yard and I will never forget the morning I stood up out of bed in front of my little basement window that looked out to a part of the side of the house where I'd never once gone myself or seen anyone else and there was Rosey right in my window, cleaning up leaves and waiving and smiling at me. This would be less memorable had it not been for the fact that I was completely naked. Rosey never let anything embarrass her though, it just wasn't her personality, she could not have cared less and never even mentioned it. I, on the other hand, invested in some curtains shortly thereafter.

Having Rahne right upstairs from us for that year in Baraboo was so nice. She was right there by our sides for the months leading up to our wedding, helping with all the planning and making of centerpieces and all the details. She was there keeping me company when Jamie would be making the long drive home from work and would stay and visit with both of us many nights. We'd watch our favorite shows and enjoy just being together. We'd sometimes go out a bar or two on the main street in the little town, but most often we stayed in our little place and hung out. I believe it was around this time that she met Jeff, who is now her husband. They would eventually buy a house together in Baraboo and we see them quite often still, making time for get togethers and camping together in the summers.

Those days when we lived together were a lot of fun and a lot of laughs. I remember one time Jamie was on his way home from work and Rahne and I decided to go get a glass of wine at a little wine bar in town. One glass led to several and I think we eventually walked next door to a bar where we had more drinks and probably played pool or darts. Time got away from us a little and I remember a call from Jamie, who had arrived home to a locked door and no key. I was always home back then so he never took a key with him. We almost never locked the door either unless we were all going to be gone at the same time. I will never forget putting Jamie on speaker phone and Rahne and I, having had one too many drinks and finding everything to be hilarious, trying to contain our laughter and composure as we explained that he'd need to come get us at the bar to get the key as we couldn't drive home. Luckily Jamie was a good sport and much needed designated driver at that moment and promptly came to get us.

Rahne remains one of our nearest and dearest friends today and we are both so thankful she is in our lives. Jamie met her years before I did as a co-worker at one of several hotels he worked at in the years before he met me. They have quite a few stories of their own from that time but I will leave those for their own memoirs. Though perhaps to persuade either of them to write theirs someday, I will tell you that I remember one of their stories involves a hotel room, a hot tub, soaking wet work uniforms, and an unexpected crossing of paths with Rahne's mom. A story for another time.

Left to right: Me, Rahne, and Jamie.

Taken on our wedding day

Chapter 28

Five for the Farm

After one full year in our little studio apartment, now married and with better incomes, we were ready for our next adventure. We had a pretty big circle of friends then and spent a lot of time with all of them. We'd been talking with a few of them about the idea of finding a big place to rent all together. We all spent a ton of time together and loved the idea of sharing one big space. In February of 2015 our idea came to fruition.

We'd found the perfect place. A huge double house of sorts set on 40 acres of farm land outside Madison. It was much closer to Jamie's work and the set up couldn't have been more perfect. The original house was built into a hill and the owners, rather than remodel, had chosen to build a brand new house right in front of it, but still connected seamlessly by a hallway. It was a unique design but perfect for our needs. Jamie and I a newly married couple would set up in the original house, complete with its own 2 bedrooms, bathroom, living room, and kitchen. Our friends, a single guy and a married couple set up in the bigger newer part in the front, which also had its own 2 bedrooms, 2 bathrooms, kitchen, and living room.

I remember wishing Rahne could have been one of the friends to join us as it was hard to leave our close quarters with her, but she was moving on with her new boyfriend Jeff and it was time for us to move on as well.

The farm house as we called it had a huge wrap around deck, a giant man made pond, a large storage shed, and 40 acres of land to roam around on with a 4 wheeler we'd gotten from my brother-in-law.

While living there with our friends, we had some memorable adventures. There was the time we invented "mattress boating", which consisted of tying and old Jon boat to the back of the 4 wheeler and putting an old mattress on top of it. Then 1 or 2 of us would jump on the mattress and someone else would drive the 4 wheeler full speed ahead through 40 acres of tall grass, corn, open fields, and the occasional prickly bush one was supposed to try to avoid. I remember one time, Jamie's sister coming to visit and wanting to give it a try. I also remember spending a LOT of time pulling weeds out of her hair.

There was an old broken pool table in the basement of the house and the landlords gave us permission to get rid of it however we could. Naturally we chose to sit it over our fire pit in the front yard, fill the pockets with fireworks, douse it in gasoline and shoot roman candles at it. I wish there was a way to share a video in a book because that one is pretty fun to watch!

We cut down our own Christmas tree that year, right from our own front yard. We blew up a microwave (safely – sort of) in an experiment fueled by both boredom and curiosity. I also remember using my truck (oh ya, I changed vehicles again, I wasn't kidding when I mentioned my problem with changing vehicles constantly in an earlier chapter) to pull a giant stump from the woods into our front yard where we turned it into a planter with our house number on it. We spent a lot of time together with our friends in those days and while a lot of people around us thought it was strange to live together with so many people, we enjoyed it a lot.

In the summer of 2015 we were preparing for our traditional get together with our entire friend group at the Lake House (a common gathering spot for our group of friends every summer – owned by the parents of one of the friends). The timing ended up working out that we'd be at the Lake house for our 1 year wedding anniversary. Since the traditional one year anniversary gift is paper, we weren't planning any sort of big celebration and decided it might be nice to spend it with friends relaxing at the Lake. I don't remember the gifts we got each other, but there was a bigger gift for both of us that we will never forget.

Chapter 29

Technically, Legislation Counts as Paper Right?

I will never forget the morning before our anniversary. We were sitting outside the lake house looking at the beautiful water, surrounded by friends, when one of our friends noticed a "sundog" in the sky overhead. If you've never seen one, it's really quite spectacular. I don't recall having seen one prior to that day myself. It's basically a rare occurrence that causes a perfect rainbow circle in the sky.

As we were looking at it, all of our phones started blowing up with breaking news notifications. The US Supreme Court had issued a ruling officially recognizing Gay marriage on the national level! What an incredible feeling that was. At this point, though we were legally married, there were exceptions in the state we lived in still. Our marriage was recognized in part, but there were certain things we still couldn't do, like add Jamie to my health insurance plan and a few other benefits we'd wished we could have had that past year.

I will never forget the countless messages that came flowing in to our Facebook pages from friends around the country congratulating us and referring to the legislation as an anniversary gift like no other for us! So many messages of that sort in fact, that to this day some people think our anniversary is the 26th, but it's actually the 27th, the day after the legislation passed.

Looking back on it now, I sometimes can't believe there was ever a time when it wasn't legal. It seems so natural and obvious to me, but so many then and unfortunately still today, believe it's wrong. We've certainly come a long way though as a nation on this topic and I had come a long way myself. From the boy in the small town who thought he was the only gay person in the whole world, contemplating suicide, terrified of what his life would look like in the future, to the Man in his early 30's, sitting next to his Husband, watching his dog play in the yard and celebrating gay marriage legislation with a great group of people who loved and supported us.

We will always remember that day as one of the times in our life when we felt more included, supported, heard, and loved than ever before. For a lot of people, that day was probably noteworthy at best, or maybe upsetting to many as well. But make no mistake that there were a LOT of people in this country that remember that day as more than a brief news headline. It made so many of us feel like we could finally breathe and feel equal to everyone else. Of course it also meant Jamie and I needed to find a new road trip game since our old one "Are we married in this state?", was not an option anymore.

Chapter 30

Two Tickets to Paradise

It was a typical weekday evening sometime in March at the farmhouse with friends. All of us wrapping up our workdays around the same evening hour and relaxing in front of the TV in the front room. You would think with 5 different people sharing the same place that there would be more of a fight over what to watch but what I remember most about those days was that the TV was always just sort of on in the background and none of us really watched it. We mostly talked about our workdays and shared funny things we saw online that day.

This particular evening the TV landed on an episode of House Hunters, Caribbean edition. For some reason, all 5 of us ended up intrigued by the episode. The host was explaining that they were on the island of St. Croix, one of 3 islands that made up the U.S. Virgin Islands. I remember all of us watching in awe of the gorgeous turquoise ocean scenes and the brightly colored homes. At one point during the show I remember turning to Jamie and saying "why do we live in Wisconsin?!" Those 6 words, though meant mostly in jest, would turn out to shape the trajectory of our lives for the rest of that year.

The next two months would consist of further and further discussions among our group of friends about the feasibility of picking up and moving our lives more than 2,000 miles away and living on a small island in the Caribbean. I had a remote work job already so the feasibility for me was pretty high, but the rest of the group were all still working jobs that required them to be in-person. I honestly don't recall all of the specifics that led up to the final decision, but I will never forget stepping off that plane for the first time in early May and onto the island of St. Croix, USVI. We'd discovered in our planning that resort stays were expensive and short term leases for homes were common and much more affordable. Though we'd planned to only go for a week to check it out, it was still cheaper to rent a house for an entire month than stay at a hotel for a week. The first visit to the island was meant to be a scouting trip, see what it's like and find out if we really want to pull the trigger and move our entire lives there. I remember thinking that it was a win win either way. If we decided not to move, we still got a weeklong vacation on a Caribbean island!

I will never forget the drive from the St. Croix airport to our rental house. The views were spectacular. The ocean really was turquoise and the homes really were bright pinks, blues, oranges, and more. The local people were never in a hurry, for anything. It was an entirely different world, a slowed down, peaceful, go at your own pace, live, and let live world, the likes of which none of us had ever experienced. We reached the gate at our rental home and it opened to reveal a charming little 3 bedroom home nestled into a hill and just a short walk from the most stunning waters we'd ever seen. The shared living space was smaller than the farmhouse but open and airy. The 3 bedrooms were all nice and the front covered porch would turn out to be the place where we spent most of our time when we were there. I don't recall if it was day 2 or 3 into our week long trip when we all agreed, but we found ourselves signing on the dotted line to extend our lease on this little house for 6 months!

The next month was a frenzied blur. Back at the farmhouse after our one week excursion to the Caribbean, we were in a constant state of planning. Everyone was figuring out finances and job situations. We were testing out doggy medications for our pups to be comfortable on the long flight. We were selling everything we owned that wouldn't fit into the few bags we allotted each of ourselves to take. We sold furniture, clothing, bikes, cars, sailboats, you name it. I remember how strange it felt to see things we'd spent years collecting being loaded into strangers vehicles and the constant revolving door of people driving out to the farm eager to buy our things. I remember also being worried about how it would ever possibly all come together and then thinking back, as I did often, to the time I sold everything and moved to Florida in my early 20s. I mentioned in that chapter how many times that life experience would resurface for me and I meant it. There was a calmness I was able to find within myself during this time once again of big change and I owe it to my younger self for proving to myself that it was something I could do.

On June 27, 2016, mine and Jamie's 2nd wedding anniversary, we were on a late night flight, our one-way tickets to paradise. I remember looking at him and wishing him a happy anniversary and saying "I hope you weren't expecting a gift, I assume moving to paradise is our gift to each other". He laughed and agreed that was more than sufficient. I don't recall the specifics of why the others didn't join us until a few days later, likely to do with jobs or final details of remaining items to sell, but that first couple of nights in the home on the island were just Jamie and I.

The days, weeks, and months that followed would not disappoint. The memories we would make together on that island, the people we would meet, the once in a lifetime experiences are almost indescribable. There is something about not just the beauty of the island of St. Croix, but the way it makes you feel, every single day. It wasn't long before we started to understand why the locals never seemed to be in a hurry. Being surrounded by such spectacular views every day has a way of making one pause, slow down, and think about what's really important in life.

We had a LOT of laughs there too. I remember the time we were all very excited about a new food cart vendor on the island. Being a pretty small place, anything new is always welcomed and exciting. We were waiting in line to order and when it was finally my turn I approached the cart ready to recite my order when the young woman behind the counter gave me a look of horror. I remember looking over my shoulder and trying to understand her scrunched up face and what she was looking at. She wasn't talking so I finally just started to provide my order when she leaned out of the food truck toward me, reached out her hand and without warning grabbed, yanked, and successfully plucked out a very long, ear hair from my left ear. Now first of all, who does that to another person, much less a complete stranger, second of all in case you are not aware, pulling of an ear hair HURTS A LOT! I was so stunned. The only thing that broke my trance of confusion was the eruption of laughter from my husband, who was behind me in line. I believe the young woman said something along the lines of, "sorry, you can order now, I just couldn't concentrate until that thing was gone". I thought Jamie was going to pass out he was laughing so hard. I was still standing there in shock and honestly can't remember if I ever did order anything or not.

Then there was the time we went to the one and only little casino on the island. Jamie loves rewards cards, coupons, point earning punch cards, and all things that make him feel like he's "getting a deal", so naturally he insisted we visit the club card membership counter right away to get signed up. I remember we approached the desk and a mid-40's woman looked at us from her seat well behind the counter with a look of defeat that she had a customer. She approached and was pleasant nonetheless and asked how she could help. Jamie explained our desire to get club rewards cards and the woman sighed and suggested it was not worth it for a brief vacationer. Jamie explained we had moved here and that set about a 20 minute conversation between the 2 of them, most of which I didn't hear as I lost interest and wandered off at one point. When I returned I will never forget the look Jamie gave me as I approached, it was that sort of "you won't even believe what's happening right now" look. I could tell he was doing everything in his power to summon his patience. As I got closer I discovered the woman, with Jamie's license propped on her keyboard, typing in his information for his rewards card at a pace that I can only describe as similar to the sloth character that plays the receptionist on that kids movie. I could tell the woman was struggling to read the information on the license and squinting her eyes between each painfully slow hunt and peck of a single key on her keyboard. I remember I said to her, "looks like you're having a little trouble seeing there" to which she promptly replied, "well if I had my damn glasses". Jamie and I both felt bad that she must have either forgotten or recently broken her glasses and both summoned our patience further.

The next 10 minutes or so she continued to hunt and peck at her keyboard before finally handing Jamie back his license and declaring his card would be popping out of the machine shortly. She then turned to me and asked if I needed anything and I reluctantly handed over my license and asked for a rewards card. The woman takes my card and says "oh lord, another one"... then she leans back in her chair and hand to

GOD, I am not kidding you, she yells loudly into the back somewhere behind the scenes of the rewards desk "Londa! Would you bring me my damn glasses!". Jamie's head slowly swiveled toward me with eyes wide and jaw dropped, and I lost it. Couldn't help it, I laughed till my side hurt. Just when I thought I had regained my composure Jamie was handed his club card which he promptly showed to me, he was now the proud owner of a rewards card with the name James Randy on the front.

We both remember fondly, a gas station attendant on island that we had come to love so much. There were quite a few gas stations on the island but there was one in particular that we had come to favor over the others. It was the only one that offered full service. Royce was always right out front ready to pump our gas for us. We learned quickly that there are times of day when even a brief time outside can be a bad sunburn the next day. Also, when it rains there, it's not like the rain we experienced back in Wisconsin, it would come down in buckets, completely drenching everything in its path. Having a full-service gas station was a huge benefit for those times when you wanted to stay in the air conditioned vehicle or avoid the buckets of rain. Royce was so friendly and always greeted us eagerly when we'd pull in. I'd hand a 20 out the window and he'd pump the gas and then we'd tip him a few bucks every time. We knew it cost a little more that way, but it was more than worth it.

One night we were out at a favorite local bar and restaurant for bingo night (another fun tradition we'd grown accustomed to on our little island). While there, we ran into some friends of ours that we'd met on island when we first moved. They joined us for a drink, and we were visiting and catching up. They'd been living on island for a few years and been giving us helpful tips on acclimating to life there. I remember mentioning to them how much I liked the full-service gas station on the east end. They both looked at each other confused and back at me inquisitively. I described the station further and then described Royce, the attendant. They both erupted in laughter and Jamie and I looked at each other confused until finally they explained to us that there are no full service gas stations on island.

As it turns out, they'd further explain, that Royce was not an employee of the gas station but rather a homeless man that tricks tourists into tipping him to pump their gas. Feeling a bit embarrassed but mostly amused, we quickly clarified if he keeps just the tips or if we'd been technically stealing gas all this time. We were assured he only keeps the tips; the gas station owner is aware of him and just sort of looks the other away so long as the customers don't mind. We decided to keep going there and tipping Royce anyway and over the next few months would occasionally help him out when we'd see him around town. Sometimes with food, or a ride somewhere. I wish we could have done more for him, but I felt good that we did what we could at the time.

For all the funny stories and incredible moments, we had in St. Croix, life is still life and there was a scary reality we would soon have to face. While we were snorkeling in the Caribbean and watching the fire dancers perform at the endless festivals and parties, back in the states, trouble was brewing, and we had no idea what we were about to be faced with over the next few months.

Chapter 31

A Preemie and a Plane Change

Back home, Jamie's little sister was struggling through her first pregnancy. A type 1 diabetic from childhood, the typical pregnancy path was not the same for her. She had many more doctor's appointments than usual and had to be so careful to maintain her own health throughout the duration. I remember Jamie's Mom being so fraught with worry throughout that entire time. Then one night in late July, almost 2 months before her due date, Jamie's sister Sarah went into labor. They tried everything to stop it or slow it down, but little Darrin was ready to greet the world, and that he did. I remember Jamie and I both wanting to be there right away, but Sarah assured us it was best to wait until he was released from the NICU (neo natal intensive care unit). I remember long conversations with Sarah over the next month, video calls, and late-night texts. She spent every waking moment by Darrin's side in that hospital. Exhausted and doing her best to keep her own health together, she was strong and there for her baby, and we were so proud of her.

It wasn't until late August that we finally got the green light that Darrin would be going home for the first time, and we booked a flight to go and meet our new little nephew. Plans changed after our flight was booked and it turned out he wouldn't be getting to go home yet, but we kept our flights and decided we would meet him in the NICU.

As was quite common with flights off our little island, there were not a whole lot of choices. There was almost never a direct flight to any destination we needed, so changing planes was pretty much an inevitability. This particular trip had more than one delay and more than one plane change if I remember right and Jamie and I arrived at the hospital in Northern Illinois in the wee hours of the night, exhausted, and looking like we'd traveled by horse or possibly been dragged behind one.

Because of the hour, the only allowable entrance into the hospital was through a security guard staffed booth at the emergency entrance. Tired, and looking it, Jamie and I made our way to the little booth and stated the reason for our visit. I remember Jamie provided details of who we were there to see and that we needed to be granted access to the NICU. The security guard pulled up some information on his computer, provided us directions and while he was waiting for our guest badges to print he said to Jamie, "so you must be the proud grandpa!" Now I should tell you that my husband has a bit of a baby face and has most of his life been accused of being younger than he is while I am usually the one in the situation of being mistaken for older than I am. That being said, you can't blame me for relishing in this particular moment a bit. I watched as Jamie stood there completely stunned and did my level best to keep my face from revealing my pure glee.

We walked to the elevator and stepped on, the doors closed, neither of us having said a word to each other at this point. I was feverishly texting on my phone when Jamie snapped out of his stunned state and turned to me and said, "not a word to anyone". To which I promptly showed him that I had already texted this bit of news to his Dad, Mom, sister, and most of my family. In my defense, a few years before this, after having his wisdom teeth removed, I picked Jamie up from the dentist and the dentist and receptionist both thought I was Jamie's father. Jamie had yet to let me live that one down, so it seemed only fair that I return the favor.

Eventually we reached the NICU and would meet and hold for the first time the tiniest, sweetest little creature. He looked so much like Sarah and was so perfect. We fell in love with him immediately and as I type this I am happy to report that he is today a healthy, happy, thriving little man who recently started Kindergarten.

Back on Island, a little jet lagged, but happy to be back in paradise, we settled in for Island life to resume. We shared pictures of our new little nephew with our friends and warned them about how hard it is to get used to driving on the right side of the road again when back in the states. It had taken us months to get used to driving on the left on our little island and it was a hard habit to break for the brief time we were back stateside. Life plugged along for the next several weeks. We learned of Moko Jumbies (costumed performers on giant stilts) and the many uses for mango from something called *Mango Fest*, there were a LOT of festivals at any given time there. We had more bingo nights and explored more beaches with our snorkel gear. Life was good and we were taking it all in one day at a time. Then one night in September, I got a call from my Mom.

Chapter 32

The Longest Flight

I hung up the phone and walked out of the bedroom and into the living room. No one was there so I continued out to the front porch where Jamie and our friends were sitting around the grill discussing how best to make kabobs. Jamie saw the look on my face and immediately asked me what was wrong. My mom had called to tell me that my Dad was having chest pains and he was in the emergency room where they'd confirmed he'd been experiencing a heart attack and would be needing emergency open heart surgery at the VA medical center in Minneapolis, MN. Jamie rushed to the computer to find the quickest flight off the island. I remember how hard he tried to get me the red eye, but everything was booked. I was panicking, we were looking at all options, a quick boat ride to Puerto Rico maybe, then fly out from there? There was nothing until the next morning, nothing.

Defeated and terrified, we booked the flight for the next morning. A couple of hours later, I escaped back to the bedroom to have a video call with my Dad. All my siblings were there and my Mom. There was Dad, lying in a hospital bed, machines all around him, knowing he was going to be going into a very scary and dangerous surgery soon. He smiled at me and said "there, now all my kids are here". We talked for as long as he had energy, which wasn't very long, and he told me he loved me, and he would see me when I got there. I remember walking out of the bedroom and falling into Jamie's arms. I had no idea if that moment was my last with my Dad or not. I was overwhelmed with fear. Jamie let me cry in his arms and then began to cry himself. He loved my Dad very much too. We sat and cried and waited with excruciating impatience for the next morning to come so I could get on that flight and get to my Dad.

The next morning, I boarded the longest flight of my life. Moments before I got on the first flight, just before I would be told I have to shut off my phone, my sister Katie called and told me Dad was out of surgery. They did a quadruple bypass, and the next 24 hours would be critical, but he made it through the hard part. I was so relieved but still had this feeling of heaviness and fear and just wanted to get there as soon as I possibly could.

My first flight was a short one, from St. Croix to Puerto Rico. Because of the last-minute booking, the only thing I could get included more plane changes than I'd ever done for a single trip. After opening what I thought was a piece of string cheese that turned out to be a tube of pudding that sprayed all over my clothes in the Puerto Rico airport (my high school Spanish failed me a bit on that one), I boarded flight number 2 from Puerto Rico to Miami. After a long wait I finally flew from Miami to Atlanta, a flight with more turbulence than I've ever experienced made all the more fun by the large man next to me spilling his entire soda in my lap. From there it was another delay for some mechanical issue and the finally it was wheels up from Atlanta to Chicago.

If you've not been to O'Hare international airport in Chicago before then this next part may not seem like a big deal to you, but I arrived at a gate in the A terminal I think it was and was departing from a gate in the D terminal I believe. All I remember for sure is that these two gates were not even in the same damn zip code, and I had 10 minutes between flights thanks to the delay in Atlanta. To this day I don't know how cart people get a cart person to drive their fancy cart asses where they need to go, but I didn't have time to explore bribery options, so I ran like I've never ran before.

The gate attendant was closing the gate as I approached and opened it for me, scanned my ticket and told me to hurry. Hurry, she said… like my complete out of breath near pass out demeanor wasn't clue enough that I was familiar with the need to hurry already. From Chicago it was finally on to Minneapolis where my sister Katie would greet me in the wee hours of the morning to drive me the rest of the way to the guest quarters next to the hospital.

I will never forget finally walking into Dad's hospital room and seeing all those machines and tubes. It was so overwhelming. After all, this is a guy who used to let all 6 of us kids climb him like a tree, at the SAME TIME! Then he'd goofily stomp around the house trying to shake us off like leaves and we'd all laugh our little heads off. This was my Dad, the strong leader of our family, laying there looking so small and helpless and pale. I held his hand and told him I loved him, and the nurse told me it was time for me to leave. I walked out and there was Mom, open arms, ready to hug me and reassure me everything would be ok. She was right, though it was a long road to recovery, my Dad did exactly that, he recovered.

I was so thankful that my sister Katie had pre-planned a trip with her best friend to visit Jamie and I on island later that week. This was all in motion well before we had any idea about Dad's condition of course, but it worked out that Dad got to go home around the same time Katie would be heading to St. Croix and I was able to join her and her friend on the same flight back to my island home.

Katie, her friend Angie, and I were greeted at the airport by Jamie, island cocktails for each of us in hand. Knowing Dad was going to be ok and having my sister there to share my little island with was a much-needed relief from the stress of the week preceding. We spent the next several days showing our guests all the island has to offer and making more wonderful memories before they had to head back. My favorite was trying to teach them how not to swallow half the ocean when snorkeling, we got some pretty hilarious pictures from that one!

My sister Katie always had and still has this way of knowing when something is off for me, and I remember before she left for home that she asked me if everything was ok between Jamie and I. I told her it was but I knew that he and I had been struggling a bit though at the time I wasn't sure exactly why or what, but she wasn't wrong that something was a little off. With all the drama back home, our island life seemed like the calm escape from it all, the slowed down perfect paradise, but the truth is, Jamie and I were in some trouble, and we had no idea just how much.

Chapter 33

We Need to Talk

Like any relationship, Jamie and I had our fair share of disagreements. In the early years it was mostly little getting to know each other's habits kind of things. He often leaves his shoes and socks around the house, and I never remember to remove hangers from the bathroom hooks and put them back where they go. We had bigger arguments of course, where to live, which job to take, whose family we spend more time with. I'd say we were a pretty typical married couple really. We fought over finances and all the usual things. One thing we were always pretty good at though, was talking it out. Sure, sometimes it would start as shouting, but over time we learned to cool down first, talk second.

When we first moved to the farmhouse with all the friends, something changed in our dynamic and I can only describe it today because we learned it looking back. At the time, we had no idea. Jamie and I got ourselves into a sort of unhealthy pattern after a while in which we would put our disagreements on hold or backburner in favor of spending time with our friends. Imagine you are having an argument with your spouse, but you have friends coming over for dinner in 15 minutes. You agree to put the fight on hold for now and discuss later. Well in our case, we got pretty comfortable putting everything on hold because we had built in friends around all the time. It was so great at the time but looking back, we realized where we started to go wrong. After all, every marriage would seem pretty great if you never took the time to hash out your arguments. We put them on hold repeatedly. Not just arguments either, things we should have been talking to each other about, our hopes, fears, dreams, we sort of got into a routine of not talking about anything too heavy and just enjoying an endless night of having friends over. When we added in the dynamic of a beautiful island, we didn't realize it at the time, but we would also put arguments on hold so as not ruin what honestly felt like a perpetual vacation. I am sure other couples have experienced putting an argument on hold or letting something go because they were in a beautiful place on a beautiful vacation, and they didn't want to spoil it. Although we were living there, it always felt a lot like vacation, and we didn't really realize we were treating it that way.

Don't get me wrong, I still wouldn't change our time at the farmhouse or on island with our friends for anything, they are amazing, and we all learned a lot from each other in our times together, but Jamie and I missed a few warning signs that my intuitive sister picked up on in less than a week with us on Island.

Toward the end of our island adventure, Jamie, and I both learned just how dangerous our new dynamic had become. We had gone so long without really connecting with each other about anything important that we had opened ourselves up to some unexpected vulnerabilities. I found myself one night, exchanging text messages with a man that was clearly flirting with me and I was flirting back. I was waiting for Jamie to get done with work and join me at our favorite bar and when he arrived I promptly showed him the texts. This would have been a good moment for him to fight with me about it but I presented it as harmless and after all the first thing I did was share it with him so obviously it was nothing to worry about. Looking back though, I think part of me was disappointed that he wasn't seemingly upset by it.

It was a few weeks later that I learned Jamie had exchanged some messages with someone else who had been flirting with him as well, the big difference being, he didn't tell me about it. I was so upset when I learned of it from someone else and I assumed it was so much worse than it was because he hadn't told me the truth or shared it with me. I remember confronting him, I remember a shouting match, and then it happened. The BIG FIGHT. Just like that, all those small things we had neatly tucked away or put on hold for all this time came crashing down around us. It was overwhelming. It was terrifying. Never had we had such a fight, not like this. This fight was different, this fight felt like it was too big, too awful. I booked a plane ticket the next morning. One ticket. One way. I left the island.

Chapter 34

More Flights, Fights, and Sleepless Nights

I was back in Northern Wisconsin staying with my parents. I had gone to the state park to clear my head and I was standing on a pier looking out over the water when Jamie came walking up behind me, crying. Turns out he'd gotten the next closest flight off the island almost right behind me. He was not willing to let me go without a fight, and I am very thankful for that.

Standing together on that pier, Jamie hugged me. We asked ourselves how the hell we got to this point and just cried together. This wasn't our dynamic, and we suddenly felt like there was this huge space between us and we were both looking at each other from so far away and wondering how we got this far apart without noticing it until now.

Looking back, I am thankful things went down the way they did. Though it was beyond stressful at the time, it was a wakeup call that we both needed. We decided to move back to WI, just the two of us, and start over, reconnect with each other, and stop putting all our problems on hold.

While it turned out to be the best decision for our marriage and I'd do it again in a heartbeat, it was hard to leave that island and I do regret the strain it put on our friends. While we all had an agreement before we moved to the island that any one of us could leave at any time if they wanted to, I know looking back that they didn't expect that to happen anymore than we did. Our single friend wasn't loving island life and moved back around the same time we did, but our married couple friends decided they wanted to stay. They were able to find a new place and make it work for a while but would eventually become what I believe is called "digital nomads", living a life of travel, and working from wherever they are in that moment. We lost touch with them for a while but have recently been talking more and it sounds like they are loving the wandering travel life.

During this time of transition and turmoil in our marriage, the difficult life moments to face would wait for no one and no problem. In the same week that we flew back to the island to collect our things and tie up loose ends I'd get a call that my Grandmother on my mom's side had passed away. I'd end up having to leave Jamie on island alone for the final few days of the trip to wrap up everything on St. Croix while I took yet another red eye off our little island to make it home for the funeral. In a seemingly too cruel and almost unbelievable twist of fate, my Grandmother on my father's side would end up passing just two short months later. By this time, there'd be no flights to coordinate as we were officially back in Wisconsin and getting our relationship sea legs stable again. It was a very stressful and heavy time, but we made it through it together.

Sharing the parts of my marriage that haven't been perfect is incredibly hard for me. In an era of social media, when we all share our vacations and our nice anniversary messages and cute pictures of our happy lives, we don't often share the difficult moments. For me, I think it's even harder as I've always felt an additional pressure beyond just my wedding vows, to make my marriage work. After all, for the first part of our relationship, marriage wasn't even an option for us, and you'll remember it wasn't legalized nationwide until our 1 year anniversary. I don't believe anyone other than myself put this pressure on me, but I always felt like I owed it to the gay community to make sure my marriage lasted. There were still far too many people that were against it and who believed marriage between two men could never work. I guess I always felt like I just couldn't risk proving them right. It was a lot of pressure to put on myself and I would realize as time went on that I didn't owe anyone anything. All that mattered to me was the commitment I'd made to my husband the day I said, "I Do" and it was important to me to work on making my marriage stronger every day.

During this time I also took a lot of comfort in knowing that my parent's love story was not perfect. I took comfort in knowing they had tough years in their marriage and persevered. Sometimes when going through hard times it can seem impossible to understand why. That age old question, why do bad things happen to good people? Awhile back, I came across a short video clip wherein someone posed that question to a reverend. The response was "I asked God for strength, and God gave me difficulties to make me strong, I asked for wisdom and God gave me problems to solve, I asked for courage and God gave me dangers to overcome, I asked for love and God gave me troubled people to help" Here I was nearly 3 decades later taking comfort in the struggles I recalled my parents having and watching them grow stronger and more committed in their marriage because of it. I am sure they didn't know when they were struggling at the time that someday it would be exactly what their son needed to have the hope and courage and determination to carry on in his own marriage.

The little place we lived in our first 6 months back in the states made for some good memories, reminiscent of our little studio apartment in Baraboo a few years back. If you've never heard of the town of Merrimac, WI, google it before this next chapter and read about how the locals most often travel from one side of the Lake to the other in the warm season.

Chapter 35

Rebuilding

Thanks to the kindness of Clint, a dear friend of ours then and now, we were able to move into a little house in Merrimac, WI upon our return from the island. I had already parted ways with the remote work job I'd had before the move to the island and Jamie had left his part time job on Island of course so we were definitely short on funds and thankful for the agreement we made with our friend. We'd agreed to fix up the little house, new flooring, and other minor upgrades in exchange for very cheap rent. We were living off savings at this point, and both looking for jobs. We had one vehicle, a truck that I had stored at my parents' house when we moved to island as I didn't want to part with it. We both found jobs quickly and bought a second vehicle since there would now be a pretty long commute for both of us.

Jamie's job was about an hour drive and mine was an hour and a half, so he drove the truck to work, and I took the more fuel efficient little car we had bought. If you googled Merrimac then you likely saw some info about the Merrimac Ferry. In the warm months, before the lake freezes over, the ferry runs all day long, carting vehicles from one side of the lake to the other.

If I timed it just right in the morning, I could pull up to the ferry port right as it was loading cars on my side of the lake and make it to work in just over an hour. In the winter months though, it wasn't an option, and my commute would include a long drive up and around the lake, pushing my drive to work to an hour and a half, one way. Jamie's commute was similarly affected by the Ferry, but he at least had alternate routes to get to the city he was working in that didn't include having to go all the way around the lake.

Acclimating back to life in Wisconsin, especially in the middle of winter proved to be challenging. On top of the cold weather, we were also in a small town, not terribly close to friends and family really, and were learning how to properly communicate with each other again and not put our problems on hold any more. I remember having some incredibly deep and painfully honest conversations with each other in that little house in Merrimac. We opened up to each other again, we were talking like we did back when we first fell in love.

While our relationship was getting back on track, our ability to navigate the culture shock of life speeding up again and no more "island time" (a term used to describe the slowed down pace of life on St. Croix) was hard to swallow. One of our very first early on challenges would come when Jamie was returning from a work function one night and turned into the left lane of oncoming traffic. (you'll remember that we drove on the left side of the road when living in St.

Croix), I had done the same many times since being back but had been lucky enough to catch my mistake and right it before any harm was done. On this particular night, Jamie wasn't so lucky. He side-swiped an oncoming vehicle and veered off the road, through a fence, and into a tree. The truck was totaled, but thankfully Jamie was ok. I still remember the look on the car salesman's face when I returned for the 2nd time in a month to purchase another car from him.

A couple of months later on an early morning commute to work, my little car would prove too light to make it up a hill covered in ice and snow, and I would find myself spinning the wrong direction and sliding down that road into oncoming traffic with no control or ability to stop. Eventually I would hit and scrape along a guardrail before finally coming to a stop. It wasn't long after this that Jamie would hit a deer on one of the country roads leading out to our little house and completely destroy the front end of one of our cars, I honestly can't even remember which one anymore. It was a little rough going for a while there, but we made it through it all together.

We liked our little house in Merrimac and as it turns out, we enjoyed the time we spent together in the evenings, laying new flooring, or painting or putting up new trim. We had some of our best talks while putting those boards down on that kitchen floor. And a lot of laughs too. After 6 months re-assembling both that little house and our relationship, we'd saved up enough money and were doing well enough in our jobs to move closer and cut down on both our long commutes. Leaving that little place was bittersweet for us. It was after all a place we never thought we'd be at a time in our relationship we'd never thought we'd face. The ironic and almost poetic nature of remodeling that house while rebuilding our relationship was not lost on us. A lot of blood, sweat, and tears went into both "projects" in those short 6 months, but it was time to move on.

Chapter 36

Madison: Take Two

You might remember hearing the city name of Madison in an earlier chapter from the time we tried to make a go of it there and fell pretty hard and fast. Don't think that memory was lost on either of us as we scouted for a place to live. We remembered all too well how expensive it had been for us a few years back and we certainly hadn't forgotten the day we had to move out of town during an ice storm. But here we were, ready to try it again. We both had better paying jobs this time and a better understanding of what to expect.

One of the first places we looked at was on the West side of town. It was close to everything and had checked most of our boxes for what we were looking for. A nice older woman met us out front one morning and was very excited to show us the place, even announcing to us that we were the first people to answer the ad and lucky to be seeing it first. She handed us an application with her contact information listed on top and set about to taking us through the apartment.

Part way through our tour we had arrived on the 2nd floor of the two-story apartment and our tour guide was pointing out that one of the two bedrooms was larger than the other. I recall she made a comment about how we'd have to fight over the bigger room or perhaps flip a coin. In this moment, it probably should have occurred to me that this woman may not be comfortable with the fact that Jamie and I were a gay couple, but it honestly didn't even cross my mind. Without giving it a second thought, I quickly pointed out that we were married and would be using the 2nd bedroom as a home office. What happened next was unfortunately one of those moments in life that comes with the territory of being a gay person in a straight world. This woman's demeanor completely changed, she suddenly decided to let us finish the tour on our own and announced she'd be out front. When we came back outside, still unsure of what just transpired, we expressed our interest in filling out the application. Although she had told us just minutes ago that we were the first to see the place, she promptly responded by saying "I'm sorry, the place has already been rented".

Jamie and I, of course, both knew that what she said was not true. We both knew as we parted ways and began to drive away that this cute place we were hopeful about was suddenly not within our reach. It wasn't our credit score, or our income to expense ratio, it wasn't an issue with a pet policy... it was discrimination, plain and simple and we both remember it was a pretty tough pill to swallow. Now I pride myself on my ability to forgive and forget, to be the bigger person, but this particular incident continued to bother me for weeks afterward and I just couldn't seem to get it off my mind. One day, a few weeks later, while shopping at Target and waiting for Jamie to meet me there when he was done with work, I sat down at the little wedding registry kiosk and began exploring the options on the screen. I was just passing time and appreciating a place to sit while I was waiting for Jamie when suddenly I had a flash in my mind of the email address that was printed atop the application for the apartment from which we were rejected. The email address of the woman that was so excited to meet us until learning we were gay and so quick to write us off immediately thereafter. I remembered the email because it was kind of a strange email and just sort of stuck with me for some reason.

Before I knew it I heard Jamie's voice behind me, having suddenly arrived at Target and looking over my shoulder at the computer screen he said "umm, whatcha doin?". I immediately came clean and explained that I was using the email address of that woman from the apartment we didn't get to sign her up for a lesbian wedding registry. Now I admit I was totally expecting Jamie to give me the look of shame and scold me for my childishness in this moment, but God love him, his immediate response without missing a beat was, "ooh, let me help!". I should write something here about growing up and learning to take the high road and regrets over having done this etc..

but in all honesty, I just didn't and still don't feel bad about it. It was pretty harmless as revenges might go and it made me laugh, made my husband laugh, made us both feel kind of silly and young at heart in the moment, and I can't imagine any real harm done. I can, however, imagine the look on that apartment owner's face when she got an email congratulating her on her upcoming nuptials to her lover Gertrude.

Eventually we would find a great little duplex on the east side of town and sign a one-year lease with a lovely, non-homophobic landlord. It was perfect, it had a fireplace in the living room, a nice front room with a big picture window and a tree in the front yard. The back yard was fenced in, and Georgie LOVED that, we could just open the patio door and let him race outside without a leash. We learned quickly that we would have to put an adhesive film of sorts on the bottom half of the glass patio door to make sure Georgie realized it was there after the first time he ran face first into it while returning from the back yard.

During this time, we were getting back on track financially and doing well in our jobs. Jamie was back in the hotel industry, his true passion, and I was trying something new. Instead of insurance for the first time in almost 20 years, I was working in sales, in the school supply industry of all things. I'll admit, I was pretty green, but it was fun trying something new and I adored my co-workers, it was such a fun little group of people and we worked in pretty close quarters.

The next year would bring continued progress for us financially and our relationship would continue to get stronger. We got out of our comfort zones a bit too, joining a gym and going regularly and I even joined a gay volleyball league! It was so much fun, and Jamie would always come out to watch me play and cheer me on. We made some great friends and had fun hosting post volleyball parties at our place from time to time.

Toward the end of that first year back in Madison there was talk of my company getting rid of the sales department, so I started looking for something local. My commute was still almost an hour, and I was growing tired of the long drive every morning and night. I applied for a job back in the insurance industry and in early 2018 I accepted a position with a company that I am still with today. Jamie would move on from his job at the same time and take two giant steps up the corporate ladder with the next two moves, from GM to Regional Manager to Corporate Director of Revenue and Performance. The most recent of which is his current position today.

I would go from Supervisor, to Manager, to Operations Manager, to Business Change Manager. Where I work today, the people I have met have been such a huge blessing in my life. My bosses, Trisha and Kelly are kind, smart, accomplished women. They have been there for me and taught me so much professionally. They have also managed to somehow become great friends of mine despite the fact that I know they're in charge and they will accept nothing less than 110% from me at work. My co-worker Tanya has practically become another sister to me. She listens, she cares, she's strong, smart, and empathetic. I can't imagine having navigated all the different positions at my job so far without her by my side. Rani, another amazing "Girl Boss", as the kids sometimes say, has become a dear friend as well. As I write this I am realizing just how many executive positions are held by women at my company. Not that long ago it was much less common for women to hold these types of positions and I am proud to work for and with all of them.

This time of transition in our work lives was only positive for both Jamie and I. We would end up moving to a much bigger place, upgrading our vehicles to nicer SUVs, and enjoying some luxuries we'd not had in the past. We would pick out new furniture together and we took some great vacations as well!

We went to Las Vegas together more times than I can recall. One time we took Jamie's Dad with us to do a mutual celebration of his 60th and Jamie's 35th. We've explored New York, Toronto, San Diego, Key West. We've seen Niagara Falls, the Hoover Damn, The Hemingway home. I was chosen as a contestant on the official traveling price is right in upstate New York and won a bunch of cool prizes. We rented and rode scooters all over Key West. We had drinks at the bar in Canada where they filmed some iconic scenes from one of our favorite shows, Queer as Folk. We went whale watching in Newport Beach where a large wave caused me to go flying across the deck of the boat, luckily I was enough drinks in to not feel it too much! We ate some of the best burgers of our lives at one of Gordon Ramsey's restaurants that was being run by the most recent winner of Hell's kitchen, another of our favorite shows. We've been to concerts and wine tastings, distilleries and glass blowing studios. We've been kayaking and jet skiing, and through it all, we've laughed together, grown more in love with each passing day, and often counted our blessings for the success and happiness we've found in life and with each other. We've said many times that there is nothing we can't face together, a theory that would soon be tested in the spring of 2020.

Jamie and I visiting Niagara Falls for one of our wedding anniversaries, I can't recall which one, 5th, maybe 6th?

Chapter 37

The Masks We Wear

We'd just returned from a trip to Las Vegas in January of 2020 when we first started hearing reports of a new deadly virus that was making its way across the globe. I remember thinking how scary it would be if it ended up anywhere near our area. There was a lot of misinformation about it and the country was pretty evenly divided between people that were worried and people that were not. In March of 2020 it became much more real and closer to home. At the time, I was the Manager of Operations at my company, overseeing close to 300 people across 4 offices and 3 different states. I remember when the direction came down from Executive leadership that we needed to get everyone out of the office and set up to work from home.

Now my company was not new to remote work. We had at least 10% or more of our staff working remotely already, but it was a process. Before this time, working remotely was a privilege you had to earn. There were a lot of rules and some hoops to jump through to get approved. It took time, equipment ordering and set up, signing of forms, providing pictures of your home set up and verifying internet speeds and more. Suddenly being tasked with moving 100's of people to remote work as quickly as possible was a little overwhelming. At the same time, Jamie's workplace had decided to go remote for an undetermined amount of time as well. Over the next month, my job would change drastically from my typical daily tasks to entirely new tasks such as handing out monitors, keyboards, internet cables and more. Giving crash courses on how to set up at home equipment, prioritizing people at higher risk to go home first, dealing with people that didn't want to work remotely or didn't know how they would make it work in their home environment. There was a lot of chaos at the time but with the help of a really great boss and co-workers, we got everyone home and toward the end of March, I finally went home too.

My boss and I have often joked since that time that I could write an entire book just on what it was like coordinating all those people to a move from in office to remote work. There were people that thought each device in their home needed its own dedicated "internets" as one person put it. Others that mispronounced the name of a device used to provide mobile internet in rural areas. It was called a MiFi (my figh) and I remember my boss Kelly and I losing it with laughter when someone pronounced it meefee, a term we both still use to this day to remind us of the laughter we found in the chaos back then.
Coordinating that many people with varying levels of technology skills and diverse home lives made for some interesting days to say the least. I have an entire chapter I could do on the guy we referred to then as

"pink pants", but I think I will save my stories from work life for another book!

Now throughout our years together, both Jamie and I have had work from home jobs at various times, but never at the same time. This would be a new dynamic for us. We were living in a 3 bedroom at the time. We had one room for our master bedroom, one for a guest bedroom, and the 3rd was a shared home office. In this new situation, we converted the shared home office into Jamie's full-time office and the spare room into my full time office. The two rooms shared a wall and we had to adjust to being able to hear basically everything that went on in each other's workday. We began to find it very challenging to keep our nightly routine of discussing our days over dinner since we both had already overheard every interesting part of the other's day. On top of which, being couped up all day in the house made us want to go out at night when our workday was done, but we were in the middle of a worldwide pandemic. Many restaurants closed their doors, some to never re-open. Bars did the same and in the area we lived, there was a county wide mask mandate. If we did leave the house, we had to wear a surgical mask over our face, and it was sort of an unwritten rule that one should make any trips out of the house quick and efficient and rare. We spent the next two months rarely ever leaving the house.

I recall many people sharing funny stories during this time of suddenly being thrust into 24/7 time with their spouses and the struggles they had with that adjustment. Jamie and I were no exception, there was certainly a learning curve to it. For years, Jamie and I had a system of who takes primary responsibility for which chores around the house. I was primary on dishes and Jamie has been primary on laundry for as long as I can remember. With him being home more and there being not much else to do, he was staying much more on top of his laundry duties, even to the point of sometimes getting to things too quickly, before I had a chance to set aside the dry clean only items. I very vividly remember a conversation from this time when Jamie was getting out of the shower one morning.

> Jamie "Hun, your horse hair sweater shedded onto the bath towels and now I'm covered in hair"
>
> Me "I'm sorry, my what?"
>
> Jamie "You know, that fancy sweater you wear sometimes"
>
> Me "Ahh, you mean my mohair sweater, which by the way comes from Angora goats, not horses. That's supposed to be dry cleaned, did you wash it?"
>
> Jamie "crap... ummm... no"
>
> Me "Then how did it shed onto our bath towels"
>
> Jamie "Is it just me or do you look younger today?"

Regardless of some of our new struggles, we followed the recommendations during this time and we didn't have anyone over to our home and we didn't go to anyone else's home. We missed our friends and family dearly and began having regular video calls with them as a way to stay connected. We found ways to bring some of our favorite "out of the house" activities to us. We bought a huge dartboard, just like the kind they have in bars where we used to like to go and play darts. We set up our own little wet bar next to the dart board and would play music, make popcorn, mix a cocktail, and shoot darts just like we were out at one of our favorite bars.

I missed the steak at my favorite restaurant and began ordering high end steaks online for home delivery and experimenting with different ways to prepare them to get that same restaurant quality taste. We discovered a lot of new shows to binge watch and probably drank a little more often than we should have. Based on the news stories of the time, we were not alone. Home alcohol sales went through the roof, off the charts record breaking sales. We were a nation in lockdown, and it was not going so well for most. There were so many opinions about the best course of actions for hospitals, schools, workplaces, restaurants. Through it all, people were dying, young and old. We were scared and we had no idea how long to expect it to last. I often think of this time as a time of wearing masks, both physically and emotionally. We were forced to wear a sort of façade depending on who we interacted with because opinions were so very strong. People we knew and loved for years were suddenly completely divided, some avidly and angrily on what we should be doing individually and as a nation. We wore a façade that everything was ok when talking to our parents so they wouldn't worry but we knew we were drinking more often and feeling scared and depressed.

After what we thought would be a few weeks turned into a few months, we hit a point where we couldn't handle not seeing family in person anymore. My parents lived 3 hours north of us and they had not been leaving their house or allowing anyone in but they would gladly sit in the front yard, properly socially distanced (a term that became as common as the word Hello during this time) with lawn chairs more than 6 feet apart, so their kids could come and visit safely. For most of my siblings that worked fine as they all lived pretty close. For Jamie and me it would have meant a 3 plus hour drive, leaving us only a few hours until we had to turn around and head another 3 hours back home unless we stayed in a hotel, which was ill advised at the time and causing some major problems in the hotel industry for Jamie in his line of work. One day in early June, I had an idea about a way we could visit family but stay safe.

Chapter 38

House On Wheels

It was June of 2020; the world was in a global pandemic and the United States was still pretty much in lockdown. Everyone was staying 6 feet apart, wearing surgical masks, and panic buying at grocery stores was causing a shortage on everything from water to soup to toilet paper. I woke one morning with an idea that maybe we could purchase a motorhome and have our own safe, socially distanced, little house on wheels to travel around in. This would allow us to see family but not have to be in their homes or they ours and further allow us to get out of the house and explore the world again without having to leave our own little bubble of sorts. Jamie was on board immediately and we began our search. After seeing several different candidates over a few weeks, we settled on a favorite, made our purchase and we were off! Our maiden voyage was up north to see my family.

I will never forget the feeling of finally pulling into my parents' driveway again after what seemed like forever. My Dad greeted us out front with a big smile on his face and laughed as we pulled into his driveway in a 32-foot beast of a machine with a tiny 10 pound dog standing on the dash looking out the big front windshield and wagging his little tail. Our dog, Georgie, as it turned out, was head over heels in love with having his own traveling little house. He adored our motorhome trips, getting to ride on the dash or sleep on the couch, get up and get a drink of water from his travel dish anytime he wanted. As a dog who had previously only ever ridden in a pet carrier for road trips, it was pure bliss. After that first trip, we were hooked. We spent nearly every weekend in the motorhome. Some nights we even just hung out in it while it was parked in our driveway just for a change of scenery.

During that summer, having the motorhome was one of the best decisions we ever made. We were able to see family so much more, explore campgrounds we hadn't been to in years, and enjoy nature in a very pretentious and glamorous way, which was perfect for us! We enjoyed making upgrades to it as well. The one we bought was an older model and had room for improvements. We put new flooring and a new toilet in the bathroom and a few other upgrades throughout. It was fun buying various things online for it and on occasion we'd wear our masks and brave the Camping World store to look for fun new things. The nice thing about that store was that it was so big and spread out and never very busy, so it wasn't as stressful as going to a grocery store and trying to stay socially distanced.

As winter inched closer, some restrictions were starting to be lifted in certain areas. People were feeling a bit safer as some areas were starting to see their first decreases in new cases of the virus and some people were just venturing out again because they couldn't take it anymore and were willing to take their chances. For us, seeing winter approaching was tough because we knew it meant putting the motorhome away for the season. Our little house on wheels had been a lifesaver during the summer of global crisis and it was hard to give up that feeling of being able to wander from our home again. Many a days after the first snowfall that winter were spent looking longingly out the window at the motorhome and expectantly waiting for spring when we could hit the road again.

Chapter 39

Patty Pocket

During that same summer of our newfound love affair with traveling via motorhome, we also got to see Jamie's family a lot. The place we were living when we first bought it didn't really have a good place to park it when it wasn't in use. Jamie's parents had a vacation home at the time about an hour north of where we lived, and we sometimes parked it there when we weren't using it. Jamie's dad, Jim, had fallen in love with the idea of finishing this vacation home himself. When he bought it, it was a shell of a house. The original owner had gotten the walls up and the roof on, but not much else. It would be a big project, but Jim was and is one of those guys that can do anything. He has every tool imaginable and as a mechanical engineer, he had the mind for and the skillsets to do everything from the plumbing, to the electrical, to the drywall and more.

Many a weekend that summer we would join Jim and Patty, Jamie's mom, out at the "dells house" as we called it, being located just outside the world-renowned popular vacation destination of the Wisconsin Dells. It was nice having the motorhome there on weekends in which we would work on the house. It was a comfortable place to escape to for a break and sometimes we'd even stay the weekend and camp right there at the house.

It was during this time that we started to become more and more concerned about Jamie's mom. If we back up a bit to a few months earlier when we were only interacting with anyone via video calls, I remember a conversation with Jamie after a particular call with his parents. We had both noticed that Patty seemed to be acting differently. She was sort of disconnected from the conversation and even seemed to be falling asleep sometimes. Naturally we shared our concerns and learned she'd been having some issues with a change in medications. Patty had suffered most of her life with terrible migraines and finally gotten them under control some 20 years prior to this point after finding the right medication to treat/prevent them. It seemed the medication was no longer working like it used to and the change up was a pretty big shock to her system.

Fast forwarding back to that summer, out at the dells house, Jamie and I noticed one particular weekend that Patty looked like she had lost a lot of weight. Now to understand why this would be so concerning, I should describe to you that my mother-in-law is an already very tiny person. I have lovingly referred to her in the past as Patty Pocket (a play on the childhood toy of the 80's/90's "Polly Pocket", a small little doll that would fit in one's pocket). Patty is barely 5 feet tall, and I don't believe she's ever weighed more than about 100 pounds or so her entire life. Losing any amount of weight when you already don't have a lot to work with is concerning. Jamie and I continued to express our concerns and Patty was always very good about listening and taking them to heart. She continued to see specialist after specialist but was having very little luck.

Then one day in early August Patty's health declined rapidly and she ended up in the hospital. I remember Jamie and I racing down to the hospital in Rockford, IL and being told we couldn't come inside due to the pandemic protocols. We were in the parking lot and on the phone with Jim, who was in the hospital room with her. I will never forget the fear in his voice. Jim and Patty are the type of couple that tend to tease each other a lot and like to get in little jabs about the other, but make no mistake, they have been married close to 40 years and they love each other a lot. Jim was terrified and trying to describe what was going on, but he didn't have a lot of answers. At one point we heard the alarms going off in the background and Jim was panicking and eventually the call dropped, and we were left sitting in that parking lot having no idea what was going on or if we were about to lose her.

We started making calls to family to activate what we call the "prayer chain". Both mine and Jamie's extended families are prayer people and it's not at all uncommon for us to ask for prayers from them in times of need. I remember he was calling his Grandma and I think I called his Aunt Michelle. It was a very scary time and we had no real answers in those tense moments.

Eventually we would hear back from Jim that Patty was stable again and it looked like she was going to be ok. She would be released from the hospital within a few days, one of which Jamie would spend with her as the allowed visitor for that day. As I write this she is still struggling to find the right balance and right doctors to get back to normal, she's been in the hospital again since and given us a scare more than once. It's hard to see someone you love struggle with their health, especially when you don't have a great understanding or hard and fast diagnosis. I have been so thankful for Patty and Jim these past 13 years. I know a lot of people don't get along with their in-laws, but Jamie and I have both been lucky in that regard. We both come from good families, and he gets along great with my family and I his. Jim and Patty have always been so kind and generous and welcomed me into their family as their own a long time ago.

In early November we made plans to have Thanksgiving with Jamie's family on the actual holiday and would be getting together with a smaller group of my family the Saturday after. With the pandemic, we'd been missing official get togethers a lot. For my family, we'd decided on just siblings and Mom and Dad having a get together at my brother Nick's place. No kids this time, but with just us it would be a small enough group for Mom and Dad to be on board. I remember so looking forward to sitting down to a meal with them again and was very excited for the day. As it turns out, 2020 would be the year of health scares for not just Jamie's Mom, but my Mom too.

Chapter 40

Things Mom Would Never Say

It was the Saturday after Thanksgiving, November 28, 2020, which also happened to be my Dad's birthday. Mom, Dad, my brother Nick and his wife Cathy, My sisters Katie, Jenny, and Bobbi, and me and Jamie were all at my brother's house for a joint Thanksgiving/Dad's birthday get together, our first indoor get together of any kind in almost a year.

Cathy had made a beautiful traditional thanksgiving meal with all the trimmings, and I remember a wonderful sit down meal with everyone talking and laughing. It was the first time in a long time that I had forgotten about the pandemic for a moment. For a short time that day, I didn't think about masks, the virus, the friends, and co-workers we'd lost, the country divided over a presidential election and the over politicizing of people's lives. It was a perfect day to this point, and I didn't want it to end.

After a delicious meal, as is commonplace in my family, we set about to playing various card games and board games. I remember laughing a LOT and one of the games giving me an impromptu idea for a game we'd call "things <u>blank</u> would never say", inserting the name of each of us for each different round. We'd go around the room and each right down for example things Nick would never say. Then someone would write them on a big white board for everyone to see and Nick being the subject of that round would have to try to guess which of us said what. I remember all of us laughing so hard, Mom included.

We'd made our way part way around the table with the game when it came to Mom's turn to be the subject. We all snickered as we wrote down our responses and Nick gathered them up and began writing them on the board. When we asked Mom to start to guess who said what there was this confusion that came over her. She began reading the responses and telling us that they didn't make sense because she didn't believe those things or would never say those things. It struck all of us as so odd because she'd been playing the game up to this point and understood and completely participated in the premise that the whole purpose was to come up with something the person would never say. She insisted though that we'd all gotten it wrong and as we continued to try to explain that's when something else happened.

Suddenly, just like that, it's like Mom was somewhere else. She stared off into the distance past all of us, not really looking at anything. None of us had ever seen her do anything remotely like this before and we all became very concerned at the same time. Whatever this episode was, it was brief, and she snapped back to us pretty quickly, but the reality of what just happened was not lost on any of us. Jamie and I were both especially concerned having recently gone through what we did with his Mom, and I remember discussing on the drive home some of the similarities to what we noticed with his Mom earlier in the year.

The rest of the day was pretty uneventful, we played more games, Mom stayed engaged in the process and nothing like what we'd seen earlier happened again. We didn't openly discuss it that day but the next day after we'd all gone home to our towns and lives, we had an emergency sibling video call. We all agreed that we'd seen the same thing happen to Mom and all agreed it couldn't be ignored. We discussed our own hypothesis but that just made us worry more I think. We all mostly agreed that it seemed like some form of early onset dementia maybe, or maybe she'd need some sort of memory care. We didn't know for sure but one thing we did know is that we love our mamma, and she is the greatest mom on this earth so we were ready and prepared to take whatever next steps needed to be taken.

My sister Katie was able to get Mom an appointment relatively quickly, only a little more than a week later. It was a Monday morning appointment, Katie and Dad would be going along with Mom and Katie would be reporting back to the siblings what if any results they might get that day. There was simply no preparing for what came next.

Chapter 41

December 7, 2020

I logged onto work earlier than normal that morning because I had trouble sleeping the night before. The date December 7th was already significant to me because it was my late grandmother's birthday, which I remember her telling me once when I interviewed her for a high school project called "the Good Ole days" was significant to her because her 13th birthday was marred by the bombing of Pearl Harbor on December 7, 1941. It was also the one-year anniversary of the passing of my Uncle Bob, a gentle giant of a man who I always remembered towering over me as a kid but with the kindest smile and deepest voice. He'd gotten sick the year before and we lost him rather quickly and unexpectedly.

Here I was facing another December 7th and I was worried about Mom's appointment. In my head, the worst-case scenario would be to find out that she had some sort of dementia or Alzheimer's or something else. I didn't really know the difference or much about either, but I had refused to let myself google any of the terms because I didn't want to further exasperate myself until I had some answers. I was more worried that like any typical doctor visit, we'd have to wait days for results, and I wanted answers now. I'd already waited more than a week since the incident and my mind was going crazy wondering what was wrong.

Early that morning I would get the message from Katie in our sibling group chat that would prove that my worst-case scenario was unbelievably far from the actual worst case. I walked from my home office into Jamie's with my phone in my hand. I was trembling, I had tears starting to roll slowly down my cheeks, but I wasn't crying, I was stunned, in shock I guess. Jamie's heart started to beat quickly as he got up and came toward me asking me what was wrong, but I couldn't say it. He eventually grabbed my phone and read Katie's words himself, *"Mom has a mass on her brain and a mass on her right lung"*

The next steps after that are pretty much a blur. I remember throwing clothes in suitcases and grabbing phone chargers and such. I don't remember really thinking too much about what I was grabbing, just going through the motions for the most part. I know we were out the door in record time for us and on the road quickly. I can't remember if I called Jamie's parents or he did, but one of us called them and asked them to drive to our house and pick up the dog and take him back to their house until we knew what our next steps would be. I remember being so thankful for my in-law family during this time, they were there for whatever we needed and were praying hard for my mom throughout. We were part way into our trip when another message came in from Katie saying *"they think it's lung cancer that has metastasized (spread) to the brain"* I am thankful that Jamie was the one driving at that point because while most of that day is a blur, I remember reading those words very clearly and I remember completely falling apart.

I remember on the long drive my mind wandering back through so many moments in life with my mom. I thought about the time she thought she'd won $100.00 on a scratch off ticket and how excited she was until she realized she'd read it wrong. She thought it was funny but for some reason it broke my little heart, I think I was probably all of 6 years old at the time. I thought about the first time she ever asked me to make one of the desserts for thanksgiving, declaring afterward how impressed she was and how good it was, then asking me to make it again each year. It might sound minor but it was such a huge deal to me, especially considering my mother's baking skills, to be complimented by her on that level, I never forgot it. I thought about the time when she and Dad and the siblings had come to visit us in Ohio and we watched Jim Gaffigan's comedy special together on Netflix. I could hear my mom's nonstop laughter in my head like I was reliving that moment.

My wandering mind snapped back to reality as Jamie and I arrived at the hospital, my brother Nick having driven from a completely different part of the state pulling in almost right behind us somehow. The girls were already there, and we all met in the parking lot and hugged each other and cried. Dad came out to the parking lot a short time later and I have never seen him looking so defeated and terrified. I hugged him and cried and told him we'd get through whatever was next together.

Over the next few days there would be many more tests and more answers. We'd learn that it was stage 4 lung cancer that had spread to the brain. We'd hear terms describing the tumor on the brain and in the lung as everything from big, to lemon sized, to one doctor calling it a goombah, whatever that meant. I would learn quickly that doctors don't treat all bad stuff all at once and I would become irritated by the repetitive number of times I'd be told they have to treat the acute, or most problematic issue first, one step at a time. We'd learn that the next and scariest step would be brain surgery to remove the mass and it would need to happen soon.

The brain surgery was scheduled pretty quickly thereafter, on a Sunday. Mom was allowed to go home until the surgery and the night before we all gathered at her and Dad's house. When I say we all, I mean we all. Everyone came, some stop ins, some stayed longer. All of us siblings and our spouses were there the entire evening and had a big sleepover of sorts. It was reminiscent of sharing that big old green army tent we used to camp in when we were kids. I remember Jamie and I sleeping on an air mattress in the dining room for maybe all of 3 hours before it was time to get up and head for the hospital. That entire night before we set up a camera in the corner and let it record the whole evening. Everyone sitting and talking and laughing together, surrounding Mom, and praying together and just being together.

The day of the surgery Jamie had reserved several hotel rooms at a hotel close to the hospital. Although it was the furthest thing from my mind, we were still in the middle of a global pandemic and the hospitals had very strict rules about not allowing any visitors. There would be no waiting room pacing for us, we'd all be pacing back at the hotel.

We knew the surgery was supposed to take several hours but somehow even knowing that didn't seem to ease my worry with each passing hour. Sitting in that hotel room, my mind began to wander once again back to memories of my Mom throughout my life. The time she woke me up early one morning and rushed me into my winter jacket and boots and had all my other siblings doing the same as she hurried us out the back door and as far away from the house as we could get through the tall snow. Dad had started the car in the driveway out front of the house to get it warmed up. He was getting ready to take my sister Marcy to her before school choir practice. When he started the car, the ignition had started on fire. He'd tried to put it out, but it spread quickly and although the driveway was a decent distance from the house itself, Mom was terrified of fire and wanted all her kids as far from it as she could get us while we waited for the firetrucks to show up. I remember thinking it was pretty exciting when they showed up with the loud sirens and the fire hoses. The fire was put out pretty quickly but not before a couple of the tires popped. I remember seeing our front yard afterward with little black pieces of rubber all over the white snow.

There was the time we'd gone fishing and Mom's only instruction to us kids was not to go in the actual lake and do not get wet. I don't remember who the instigator was, but I do remember riding home in our underwear on a towel in the backseat with Mom pretending to scold us the whole way. I could see her and Dad both laughing in the front seat and trying not to let us see that.

I was thinking about the time she found several half eaten stale sandwiches stashed behind my dresser in my room. She used to have a rule that I couldn't go next door to play with my friend until I finished eating. I was such a pain about food then. I was so thin, but eating seemed like a chore that got in the way of all the other things I wanted to do. Looking back I knew Mom had this rule because she was worried I wasn't eating enough. I suppose I should have known that my plan to eat a few bites and hide the rest behind my dresser would eventually backfire. I think that was the memory I was lost in at the moment when the call came into my sister's phone and jolted me back to the reality of the situation and where I was. It was the surgical nurse saying Mom was out of surgery, it had gone really well, and she was in the recovery room. They'd been able to remove the entire mass.

I remember the overwhelming sense of relief and joy in that little hotel room that we'd all gathered in all day. There were a lot of happy tears, hugging, and immediate prayers of thanks to God for our mamma having made it through. We all knew this was just the beginning but in that moment we celebrated the victory of this first and very scary step. At that time, it wasn't super clear what the next steps would even be. The only thing I knew for sure was that I couldn't stand the thought of not being there, closer to Mom and all my family for whatever the next steps would be. I knew it would be hard to navigate my need to be there as much as possible with the fact that my life and my home were more than 3 hours away. I was both happy and overwhelmed at the same time. What happened next would be a big reminder of how lucky I was to have married Jamie.

Chapter 42

A Second Home on 2nd Street

Mom was home and recovering. She had a large bandage wrapped around her head but beyond that you wouldn't have believed the woman just had brain surgery. She was up and about and active, with her walker for stability, but I have video that proves that walker was mostly just a precaution at that time. She was in good spirits, dancing down the hallway, baking in the kitchen, and feeling so much better than any of us expected.

The doctor appointments a week or so later would be where we would learn the next steps and proposed treatment plan. I was back in Madison and joined a video call with all my siblings while Katie was in the room with Mom, Dad, and the doctor. We all listened in as the doctor described his plan to use radiation treatments to address the mass in Mom's lung. I remember him explaining that Mom would need different types of radiation in the lung than in the brain. Even though the mass had been removed from the brain, there were residual cancerous cells surrounding the area in which it was removed. I remember he described how the radiation in the brain would need to be very specific, targeted, and carefully measured to the last detail because the slightest misstep could cause serious issues for her. He described radiation on the brain like trying to navigate a helicopter around the buildings in a big city and he described the radiation on the lung like dropping a big bomb on an island in the middle of an ocean. While the brain radiation was scary, he made us feel like the lung radiation would be much more aggressive and I remember writing down a lot of what he said, including "we can blast that sucker right out of there, it's in a perfect spot where there is nothing critical near it so we can be really aggressive".

They'd be starting with the radiation soon. The plan was between 5 and 8 treatments. Mom would need to travel from her little town to a place about an hour away for all these appointments and he cautioned that it could be a bit of a challenge. She'd be tired and could experience a myriad of side effects. Some were minor, some were more serious, like blood clots. He was very good about explaining everything and answering all our questions. I remember listening in and starting to cry because I wanted to be there, for all of it, I wanted to soak up as much time with Mom as I could but also help in any way I could.

When Jamie got home later that night, I was in tears again. He was worried I'd gotten bad news from Mom's doctor appointment earlier in the day and I assured him that wasn't the case. I remember telling him all about the appointment and the treatment plan and next steps. I remember him saying it sounded encouraging and hopeful and looking at me confused as to why I was still crying. I remember he held me in his arms and let me cry and said, "what can I do? Just tell me how I can help". I looked up at him and said, "find us a 2nd place to live close to Mom".

Now I will tell you that my husband, when given a task to focus on, will tackle that task like no one else I have ever met in my life. He began looking for everything from short term rentals to homes to purchase. I was still working remotely at this time, but Jamie's work had begun bringing employees back in the office part time. The logistics of how we would possibly move our lives 3 hours north were overwhelming to me, but it was the only thing in the world that I wanted, and Jamie was determined to make it happen somehow.

Two weeks later Jamie and I pulled into the driveway of a very small, older little brown house located less than 5 blocks from my parent's house. It was dated for sure, but somehow still kind of charming in its own way. The owner of the home, Chuck, greeted us in the driveway, shook both our hands and encouraged us to come on inside.

At this point in life, Jamie and I had reached a financial comfort status that allowed us some pretty nice things. Our home in Madison being equipped with the latest and most modern appliances, cabinetry, flooring, décor etc. We'd lived our fair share of places, big and small, old, and new, and the purpose of this little extra house was that it was close to my parents, so nothing else mattered. I admit we both gave each other a sideways smirk when we saw the lime green plastic cabinets in the kitchen and the large brass framed mirrors on the brown paneled walls of the living room, but the price was right, the location was perfect, and the owner didn't want anything more than a check and a handshake to hand over the keys.

I remember at one point in the little tour, we were in the unfinished basement. There was some water along the edges of the walls but didn't appear to be any structural issues. Chuck, a tall, plain-spoken man who had lived in this town his entire life and owned the local auto parts store was a very nice man from what we could gather. That said, we were still a married gay couple in a very small town. I will never forget when he, standing between us and the only exit, looked at us and said "so, umm, ahhh... you two brothers then?" Before I could even open my mouth to reply, Jamie chimed in with a resounding "Yes! Brothers.. yep!"

We wrapped up the tour, handed him a check, he handed us the keys and we parted ways. When Jamie and I got back in our car I immediately turned to him and said in my most straight guy voice ever "What's up bro?", to which he promptly replied "I panicked ok! We we're in a basement with a very tall, very straight, small-town dude, I didn't see any clear exits, I don't know, I panicked!" I remember we both sat in the car laughing hysterically for quite a while. However it came to be and whatever white lies Jamie told for possible fear of our safety, the point was we had a 2nd home, blocks from my parents, and I felt a huge sense of relief. I remember during this time, thinking back to the lady in Madison that rejected us for an apartment because we were gay and wondering if Jamie's fears weren't in fact perfectly justified, while at the same time feeling sad that it was something we had to actively keep in mind.

We'd discover later that my Uncle would clarify with Chuck, our small-town landlord, the very next day while in his auto parts store that Jamie and I were in fact married and not brothers. We also learned that my brother-in-law, Kevin with an "I" a couple days after that was also in the auto parts store and Chuck inquired with him why he thought we would have lied to him, to which Kevin promptly replied, "well look at ya!". Chuck laughed and replied with "fair enough", but it was a good life lesson for Jamie and me both. Here we were worried that we'd be ridiculed or stereotyped if we were honest about who we were, but it was actually the two of us that had stereotyped him, pegging him as small town and therefore not likely to be accepting of us. The irony was not lost on us considering the rejection we got from a woman in a liberal city like Madison just a few years prior. We were very wrong, and Chuck treated us with nothing but respect while we rented that house from him.

The next week would consist of deciding what items to bring from our Madison home to our up north "cabin" as we chose to call it. It made us both feel better about the brown paneled walls and dated nature of the home to pretend it was a rustic retreat of sorts. We would end up purchasing a few things for the home and setting up the rest with spare items we already had. We set up offices for both of us and made sure to get internet hooked up right away. We worked out a schedule with Jamie's job in which he would work in the office in Madison on Monday's and Tuesdays, then every Tuesday night after he got home from work, I would have the car packed and ready to go and we would head north to the cabin. We'd stay and work from there Wednesday, Thursday, and Friday every week and the weekend would be optional to either of our homes depending on what was needed with Mom. We had duplicate everything at the cabin, so we didn't have to pack too much each time. Georgie's food and dishes and extra clothes for us and all bathroom toiletries, extra toothbrushes, everything.

I had no idea what the next couple of months was going to look like at that time, but looking back now, I can tell you that they would end up holding some of the most important moments of my life.

Chapter 43

Late Nights and Early Mornings

It was 5:30 am on a Wednesday morning in early January. I hurried to shut off my gentle wake alarm before it got loud enough to wake Jamie or Georgie, both snuggled in next to me, closer than usual because the bed at our cabin home was much smaller than the one we were used to back in Madison. My routine on mornings at the cabin was always the same. I would get up much earlier than I was used to, shower, dress, make myself a cup of decaf in my travel mug that my niece Abby had custom designed. I would do all of this as quietly as possible to try to let Jamie and Georgie sleep in. Some mornings it worked out well and other mornings I would drop something, Georgie would bark, Jamie would sit straight up in bed and then just like that the whole house was up early!

Once my coffee was made I would put on my coat and shoes and head out the front door to my car and drive the 5 blocks over to Mom and Dad's house. Letting myself in through the garage entrance, there would be Mom, in her chair, rosary beads in hand, saying her morning prayers. She'd smile at me and ask me if it was cold out. I'd check to see if she needed more coffee or some toast and once I had her set up with what she needed then I would settle in next to her in Dad's chair, where I would stay until Dad got up in a couple of hours and then I'd move to the sofa.

A little before 8 am I would head back to the cabin to start my workday and I would always let Mom and Dad know I'd be back in a couple of hours to have lunch together. Sometimes I would be cooking lunch, sometimes we'd order out, and sometimes there were leftovers planned. When I would get back to the cabin, Jamie and Georgie would be up and into their day, Jamie logged on to his computer in the tiny little 2nd room that was big enough for a table and a chair, which was all we needed it to hold.

The living room was sort of an odd layout, which worked in our favor as there was an alcove off to one side where I was able to set up a makeshift office for myself. On the occasion Jamie and I had conference or video calls at the same time, he could shut the door to his little office and with me being around the corner in the living room, it worked out fine and we were able to go about our workdays seamlessly to anyone on the other end of the line. Although Jamie's co-workers would eventually learn that when they saw blue plaid curtains and paneling in the background it meant he was up north. I was fortunate enough that video calls were rarer for me, a bonus since during this time I was often running on very little sleep and certainly looked it.

Lunch time at my parents' house was always one of my favorite times. You never knew who would be stopping in. I remember being amazed at how Mom always had enough of literally anything and everything on hand to feed whoever popped by. My 3 sisters and all their kids lived close by and getting to see all of them so much more often was something I absolutely cherished about this time. My brother Nick lived further away like me but had made changes to his work as well to be there several days each week as often as he could. A typical lunch time routine there would consist of making a main course and several sides then continuing to sit out more leftovers and options as kids would stop in between classes at their school just up the street. My sister Bobbi worked as a nurse at the clinic that you could see out the back window of my parent's house and would walk over on her lunch break every day. It was always a time of lots of family and chaos and laughter.

After lunch I would head the 5 blocks back to my little home, usually bringing something to Jamie for lunch. Sometimes he would join me at my parents' house on the lunch hour, but most days he was booked solid with meetings, and I would just bring something back for him. On days when lunch was carry out, I'd always get the same thing for myself and Jamie from the local little diner, a grilled cheese sandwich with crispy bacon on it and a side of beer-battered French fries. This wasn't an actual menu option but one thing you have to love about small towns, if they have all the ingredients to make something for you, they will. We ordered this enough during that time and got enough of the rest of my family hooked on it that I believe it's actually now a menu item at that little diner.

When our workdays would wrap up around 5, we'd feed Georgie and let him out then he'd settle into his little dog bed for a long nap, and we'd head back to my parents' house for the evening. The evenings would be mostly spent playing cards with Mom and Dad and/or watching some of their favorite TV shows with them. I remember a lot more game show network in my life during this time for sure.

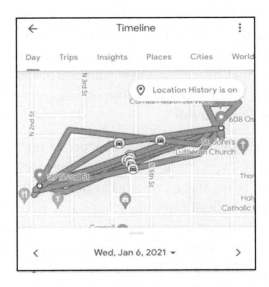

Above is an actual screenshot from my phone's location history during this time, showing our travel back and forth between those 5 blocks

Also, throughout this time there would be days where Mom had radiation treatment appointments and I was so thankful to work for a company that let me flex my work schedule around those and I would go along as often as I was able. I remember hating what she had to go through for those appointments. They made a custom mask for her that would be placed over her head to keep her still and there was a large uncomfortable belt of sorts that had to be tightened over her torso. The mask was literally placed over her face then bolted down to the table she was laid on. Even though the treatments were awful to think about, you'd never know it with the way my Mom handled everything then. She would laugh and talk the whole way there and though she was pretty weak at this time and sometimes needed a wheelchair and always a walker, she faced each appointment head on and would say "let's do this".

During this time, I recall having a recurring feeling of helplessness. I was there, getting mom her coffee, making her toast, baking cookies as per her instructions shouted from the living room on the other side of the half wall separating it from the kitchen, but I still often felt helpless. On the rare occasions Mom made any sort of special request, I jumped at the chance to fulfill it. Big or small if she wanted something, I wanted, no... I NEEDED to make it happen. I will never forget the day she was headed to one of her appointments and she had asked me to stay behind and make a chocolate zucchini cake with my special frosting recipe because she liked mine better than her own. What a woman, my mother... two birds with one stone. Making me feel needed and simultaneously boosting my confidence in my baking skills. All while she was in the battle of her life.

I remember I went about gathering all my needed ingredients and was happily starting to bake when I realized part way through that I was missing a couple of key items for my frosting. This was one of those rare occasions where Jamie was back in Madison and I didn't have a car for a couple of days. No one was home at my parent's house but me and I didn't have a way to get to the grocery store. My parents only lived a few blocks from the store but my cake was already in the oven and I couldn't leave it unattended to walk to the store. I remember I was completely reduced to tears when I picked up the phone and called my best friend Adam.

He had grown up not far from my parent's house and his mom still lived in the same town. I hoped against hope that maybe, just maybe, he'd be in town visiting his mom. When he answered and declared that he was in fact in town I cried harder. Through my tears I explained what I needed from the store and he arrived at my parent's house, groceries in hand, less than 10 minutes later. This is true best friendship. He didn't question my tears over a simple frosting because he knew that wasn't what my tears were truly about. He knew I just needed to get this right for my mom. I remember he even rolled up his sleeves and started helping me in the kitchen without being asked.

Thursday evenings were a little different routine. Each of us siblings, during this time, decided that there would be not one hour of one day at any time in which one of us would not be there, 24-7, we made a schedule. Thursday overnights were my "shift", and the day would go pretty much the same as I described the others with the main difference being, when it was time to go back to my little house and settle into bed, Jamie would go alone and I would stay on the couch at Mom and Dad's.

Now I will tell you that my Mother for as long as I can remember has always been a very early riser. She was raised on a dairy farm and used to tell me that getting up at 4am or earlier was just in her blood. But during this time of radiation treatments and post brain surgery, Mom's "up early" routine was even earlier than the 4am mornings I remembered from my childhood. It was not at all uncommon for my Mom to go to bed around 8 or 9pm and be up by 2 am, sometimes even 1 am and on rare occasions midnight. I still laugh when I think about the number of times I would fall asleep on that couch around 11:30 and anywhere from 30 minutes to 2 hours later I would wake to hear Mom coming down the hallway with her walker and headed for her chair to start her morning prayer routine. I laugh because without fail every time she would insist I go back to sleep and then continue to talk to me and ask me questions about my life and tell me stories about hers then every so often ask me why on earth I was still awake and insist I go back to sleep.

While Mom and I had always been very close throughout my entire life, I learned things in those wee morning hours that I had never known. She shared stories of her childhood I hadn't heard before. She taught me all her favorite prayers, including her most favorite one which she would actually sing. She taught me how to sing it with her, at 3 in the morning, the house quiet and dark except the one little lamp between our chairs. *"For the sake of his sorrowful passion, have mercy on us, and on the whole world"*.

The hard part about this time was when it was time to head back to Madison for a few days. It helped knowing I would be back very soon, and my little cabin home was waiting for my little family.

Friday, February 5, 2021, was like many Fridays before it. I had slept about an hour total the night before by the time Mom had woken up and we had visited the wee hours of the morning away. At this time, I had worked it out with my boss that I would be off Friday mornings until noon because I knew I would need a nap to be able to function. Sometimes I would head home in the mornings as my sisters and/or their kids arrived, but more often than not I would end up staying and visiting and foregoing the nap. That afternoon when Jamie and I wrapped up our workdays, we packed the car with a few things like usual, loaded up the dog and stopped at Mom and Dad's like we always did to say goodbye and hug them and tell them we'd be back in a few days. As it turned out, we'd be back a lot sooner than we thought.

Chapter 44

February 6, 2021

It was Saturday afternoon. Jamie and I had spent the day doing some cleaning at our home in Madison, which had been sorely neglected the past two months. We were gone more than we were home and I remember being so thankful for Dan, our amazing next door neighbor in Madison. Without being asked, he'd use his snowblower to clear out our driveway when we were away. He brought in any packages we'd have delivered and in general just kept a close on our place for us at all times. He was and is the very definition of a good neighbor.

I'd been very adamant about keeping the little cabin house up north clean, knowing that we had offered any family members welcome use of it while we were gone should they ever need it. I took out all garbage, washed down counters, cleaned and put away dishes and vacuumed right before we would leave every single week.

Back in Madison though, we were always so exhausted when we would be home for a couple days that I admit we didn't keep up with it nearly as well there. After dividing and conquering a nice once over of the house and feeling like we'd accomplished quite a bit, we sat down to watch a show and relax for a bit. That's when the message came through on our sibling group chat.

"Ambulance on the way for Mom, she can't breathe"

Once again we found ourselves on the road in record time with a few things we thought to grab and me on the phone with my in-laws again asking them to go to our house and get the dog. Messages were coming in fast as we drove, and my sisters learned more information. Mom had arrived at the ER at St. Joseph's hospital in Chippewa Falls. Shortly after that we'd learn she had developed several pulmonary embolisms in here lungs (blood clots). I didn't need either of my nurse sisters or google to tell me how serious this was, I already knew. The doctor had explained to us months before that this was one of the things that might happen and did a pretty good job of explaining how dangerous and life threatening it can be.

We drove and prayed and drove some more and prayed some more. Updates kept coming in, they'd need to transfer her to Sacred Heart Hospital in Eau Claire soon via ambulance. I remember asking my sister Katie to level with me on whether or not they thought she'd make it to Sacred Heart and while I am sure it was hard for her she relented that there was real concern she might not. One pulmonary embolism is dangerous, much less multiple. Some people never make it to the hospital, and she would need to be transferred yet again. I remember begging and pleading with God that I would be able to see her before they transferred her. We knew that the pandemic rules at hospitals at this time didn't allow much wiggle room for visitors, but we also knew that St. Joseph's was more lenient than Sacred Heart.

My brother was on course from his part of the state and tracking to arrive about the same time as us. He was driving alone so every message that came through in our sibling chat, I was then calling him and relaying the news so he would not be reading texts while driving. I remember he and I both fighting back tears when I relayed we would most likely have to go to Sacred Heart as we both knew they had strict rules on no visitors. We vowed together that the two of us would see our Mother and that was that, though we had no idea how we were going to make it happen. My sisters were all with Mom at home before the ambulance and St. Joseph's had allowed them to see her again before the transfer to Sacred Heart as well.

We were about 30 minutes out when I got a message I will never forget. Katie was with Mom and Mom kept telling her there were some things she needed to say. I can't imagine how hard that was for Katie to relay back to us, but I am so thankful for her strength during that time. She sent a message in our sibling chat of the things Mom wanted to say to all of us:

1. You need to be strong for Dad... all of you
2. The boys need to get here... that will help
3. You've all taken such good care of me
4. I'm sure about my decision on my living will, I don't want anything done, I trust the Lord.

5. You'll need to cancel a lot of appointments this week (laughing when Katie told her she'd do anything to get out of physical therapy)
6. I did so good this morning

That last one cut like a knife. She was referring to the progress she was making with her therapy exercises. She had to stand fast then sit and repeat several times, she had arm exercises she had to do and more. I had helped her earlier in the week with counting for some of them and she would smile and say, wait, I think I can do one more, and when she did successfully do one more, she would give me this "see, I told ya I could do it" grin. The part about the living will was hard to read too but it wasn't new information for me. Mom was always pretty clear on that piece and I've yet to meet anyone who had more trust in the Lord than my mamma.

We arrived at Sacred Heart to find my sisters all huddled in one of their cars in the parking lot. Nick pulled in right behind us. I went to the window to speak with the sisters, and they clarified that Dad was with Mom now in the room and the staff said no one else would be allowed in. She was stable at this point, but her condition was still very critical. Nick jumped out of his truck and made his way over to me standing by the car and talking with the sisters. He gave me a look that I knew meant, we're doing it anyway and we said, let's go. Our sisters said they'd pray for our success and in we went.

My brother and I spent the next 30 minutes shamelessly arguing with one staff member after another, all of whom were just trying to do their jobs and follow the rules. I had seen news stories of health care workers being berated for not allowing people to see their ailing loved ones but who were just doing their jobs. I didn't want to be one of those people making their jobs harder, but in that moment, I knew that all that was between me and the possibility of the last time I would ever see my mother alive was a door and couple of flights of stairs. I don't remember which manager, director, VP, or Administrator we were on or what words finally broke whomever it was that we were talking to, but after half an hour, one of the staff finally relented and gave us 30 minutes. Nick and I quickly hurried through the doors and up the stairs to Mom's room.

I remember when we walked in Mom was lying in the hospital bed and Dad sitting in the chair right next to her. She looked ok, not great, but better than I had imagined she might. The look on her and Dad's faces was sort of amused shock, since they both knew the rules were not bendable on visitors and having spent quite a bit of time at this hospital recently they knew they had yet to see those rules bent. I remember leaning in and kissing Mom's cheek and telling her I loved her. She said she loved me to then said, "how did you get in here?" I said, "don't worry about it, we're here", to which she promptly changed to her serious mom face that I recognized meant I better tell her right now. I wasn't sure how best to describe to her that we had literally just talked until we were blue in the face, and they were sick of listening to us so I asked her if she remembered how I passed my high school biology class. She got a big smile on her face and I said, "you know me, blah blah blah, can talk my way outta anything ma!" It was so good to hear her laugh. We could tell she was tired, so we didn't stay too long. We had told her we loved her and we would be close by praying hard for her and we left to let her rest.

While Nick and I were inside getting blacklisted from ever being allowed re-entry to that hospital lobby, Jamie was of course out in the parking lot scrambling to book a bunch of hotel rooms for all of us again. I was so beyond thankful for him throughout all of this. Mom was stable for now, waiting to see if the blood thinners they were giving her would break up the blood clots, Dad was with her, and the rest of us headed over to the hotel together to do our best to get some sleep and see what tomorrow would bring. I remember laying my head down on the pillow in our hotel room, exhausted and terrified but also every time I closed my eyes all I could see was Mom's smiling face and hear her laughing when I was describing how we weaseled our way in to see her. Sleep would come eventually but not easily, and it would not last very long.

The next day I only remember a little. We had made a rotation schedule for who would stay with Mom for each of the 24-hour allotments. The rules were only one visitor, and that visitor could only be changed/swapped out for someone else every 24 hours. Katie would be spending the day with Mom on Sunday, and it was my turn on Monday.

Most of Sunday passed with small updates here and there, some of the clots were shrinking but one in particular was really not responding yet. This one clot that was causing the most trouble was called a saddle clot, I assume because it literally looked like a saddle, sitting over the area in which the right and left lobes of the lung connect. This was the clot that made it so hard for her to breathe and was at present the most pressing concern of the doctors. Still, we waited. I remember thinking how strange it is that even life-threatening medical situations can still have an element of waiting to them. We sat in our hotel room all day praying, eating, watching some TV from time to time or playing on our phones to distract ourselves. Jamie ran to a department store at one point to buy more clothes for us. We'd gotten so used to having extra things in each home that we hadn't grabbed much to take with us, not thinking about the fact that we'd be in a hotel near the hospital rather than our little cabin.

My niece Miki was with us in the hotel, and I remember discussing the schedule of who would be with Mom and what days and she was sad that she wasn't in the rotation earlier due to her work schedule. She was worried she might not get the chance to take one of the days. I offered to switch with her and told her she could stay with Mom the next day, Monday and she was thankful and jumped at the opportunity. God works in mysterious ways they say, but looking back, this one wasn't so mysterious after all, I understand completely why things worked out the way they did and why Miki would end up being with Mom the next day, a day I am certain for the rest of my life, I will never forget.

Chapter 45

Code Blue

I had no idea when my niece Miki made me an Uncle for the first time at 9 years old that one day I would have more than 20 nieces and nephews and even some great nieces and nephews. I also had no idea that one day Miki would be standing in front of me as a gorgeous, smart, married, accomplished young nurse, having followed in the footsteps of so many of the women in my family. It was Monday, February 8, 2021, and my now almost 30 year-old niece was spending the day at the hospital with my Mom and relaying back information in our group chat with such deep understanding of the medical terms and the situation that I was bursting with pride.

Throughout the couple of months since Mom had been diagnosed, Miki was included in the rotation of mine and my siblings 24-7 care at Mom and Dad's house. She was there as often as she possibly could be. Having lost her mom, my late sister, at only 5 years old, Miki had developed a lifelong bond with my Mom that was more reminiscent of a mother daughter relationship. Truth be told, Miki always felt more like the littlest sister than the first niece. She adored my Mom and had been struggling with the rest of us to wrap her head around the events of the past two days and the seriousness of Mom's condition.

It was about noon when another update came through in our group text. I remember Miki's text describing medical terms but also using lay terms for the benefit of those of us not in the medical profession. *1 of the blood clots is not responding to the heparin (blood thinner). It's causing sever reduction in systolic function of the right ventricle (heart failure). They want to perform a procedure called pulmonary thrombectomy. This would entail going in through the vein and retrieving/removing the clot.*

Miki relayed that Mom had insisted that she wanted to see all of her family together and discuss the procedure together as a family before she would make a decision. You'll remember the pandemic rules of this time and how only one visitor was allowed at a time. I wish I could have been a fly on the wall to hear the way my powerhouse of a niece talked her way into allowing all of us to come to Mom's room and discuss and pray together. Somehow she pulled it off and we all headed from the hotel to the hospital.

Miki's husband Kyle had been with us at the hotel and came along to the hospital. I remember when my brother Nick and I walked into the lobby along with Kyle, we approached the lobby reception desk to see the same woman Nick and I had battled with two days earlier in our bid to see Mom the day she was admitted. She was a very nice woman and I remember feeling bad about how hard I made her job that day.

When we told her what Miki had instructed us to say upon arrival she conveyed her awareness of the exception to the rule and asked if all 3 of us were sons of the patient. In the chaos of the day it hadn't even really occurred to me as we headed to the hospital that Kyle might be turned away. Before Nick or Kyle could say a word, I immediately said, "Yes, we're all her sons". Two seconds earlier I was feeling bad about how hard I had made this woman's job recently and here I stood lying to her without giving it a second thought. She didn't press for proof, rather just giving us each a visitor pass and telling us we could head up to Mom's room. Dad and my sisters were right behind us and we all gathered around Mom and waited for the doctor.

The doctor came in a short while later and took us through everything. How the procedure would work, what they would do, what the hope was that it would accomplish, and finally, the risks. From what we understood, there didn't seem to be a whole lot of options. The clot needed to be removed and sooner was better. The nature of blood clots is that they can move at any time, and where they move to is almost always a life-or-death situation. We prayed together and discussed as a family and decided to go ahead with the procedure.

Shortly before the procedure was supposed to take place, we were all sitting in Mom's room visiting with her when we overheard on the hospital loudspeaker "Code Blue, Code Blue". A short time later, a nurse would come in and explain to Mom and the rest of us the Mom's procedure would be delayed while staff attended to an urgent stroke patient that had just come in. We instinctively all said a prayer for the patient the nurse just described even though we didn't know them. When we were little Mom always used to tell us to do the same whenever we would see an ambulance, prayer for whomever is inside. This meant we'd have some more time to visit with Mom and she was certainly not upset by the delay, especially because it was nearing 2pm and that meant her favorite prayer, the chaplet of mercy, would be sung on TV shortly on one of the religious channels she liked.

Mom picked up her remote and tuned in and then we all joined hands as a family and sang it together. For any non-Catholics reading, the chaplet follows an entire rosary which means it takes a long time, you repeat 5 sets of 10 of the same prayer, so essentially we would sing the same words over and over again together 50 times. I remember smiling and thinking back to one of our first early mornings together since her diagnosis when Mom first taught me this same prayer. At one point she had fallen asleep in the middle of a verse and then woken back up a few seconds later still singing but now at a different part of the verse. I remember jokingly telling her that verse didn't count and she had to start over and both of us laughing so hard and teasing each other back and forth. Here we were singing it all together as a family, surrounding Mom in her hospital bed, each of us probably realizing that she had taught it to all of us on our respective early mornings with her since none of us missed a beat. She looked happier than I have ever seen her and so peaceful and content in that moment. If you knew my Mom you knew that nothing made her happier than being surrounded by her family and to have us all there singing her favorite prayer with her I can imagine was a wonderful moment for her.

Eventually the doctors would come to the room to get Mom somewhere close to 5pm and they would allow 2 people to move to the waiting room outside the operating room and the rest of us would be asked to stay in the current room to wait. Before they wheeled her out of the room we each took our turns. When it was my turn, I put her hand in my hand and squeezed it, kissed her forehead, told her I loved her so much and she squeezed my hand back and told me she loved me so much too. They wheeled her out the door and Katie and Dad followed behind.

The rest of us sat and waited and prayed. I don't remember how much time passed but it wasn't a lot before we heard a now familiar call over the loudspeaker again, "Code Blue, Code Blue". I remember initially thinking another patient must have come in with a serious issue. I remember also thinking, I hope they don't have to delay Mom's procedure again, a selfish thought I know, but I was so worried and just didn't want the doctors to be distracted by anything. It wasn't until I caught the eye of my brother Nick sitting on the other side of the room and saw the look on his face that it even occurred to me that it could be a Code Blue being called for Mom. It was almost as if all of us realized that at the same time and Nick was the first to send a message in the group text to Katie and ask if she knew who the code blue was for. Moments later came her response, *Guys, it was for Mom, she's not breathing, they're doing CPR, the Chaplin is coming to get all of you, be ready to come down here.*

Sometimes I wake in a cold sweat in the middle of the night after having dreamt of running down a long hallway with seemingly no end. I wake and realize I am reliving the day I am describing to you now.

The chaplain came into the room and asked us to follow him and we ran out of the room. He stopped at the elevator, pushed the button, and when the doors didn't immediately open he ran for the stairs and urged us to follow. We went down many stairs before bursting through the doors to another hallway. As we were running I remember grabbing Miki's hand on my left and my sister Jenny's hand to my right. I remember saying through frustration and tears, "where the hell is it, how far is it?". We kept running, one hallway after another until we finally burst through another set of doors to a small waiting room where Dad and Katie were standing. All the color had drained from their faces and they told us Mom's heart stopped and the doctors were trying to get her back.

I don't remember how long we stood there before one of the members of the code blue medical team came out and told us how long they'd been trying and asked if they should keep going. I can't begin to describe to you what that question feels like. There is no right way, no right time, no right person, or situation that will ever prepare anyone for that question. I remember trying to summon the courage to say anything at all but just standing their stunned. None of us knew what to say and we all looked to Dad, who was barely standing and more shook than I have ever seen him. He looked at the doctor and said, "Go save my wife".

We all pleaded with God to save our mamma. We weren't ready, we thought we had so much more time, we needed her to make it through this. The same young woman came back out from the procedure room. Her pace was slower this time, her head was tilted down. She took off her surgical mask slowly as she approached. We looked into her eyes terrified. She told us mom was gone. Her heart had stopped. They'd done everything they could to get her back, she had fought so hard, but this was it.

My mamma was really gone.

Chapter 46

Today

It's mid October 2021 as I write this. We kept the little cabin house up north for a few more months after Mom passed and kept up the same schedule of 24-7, only now it was just to be with Dad and ensure he was never alone in that house. We gave up the cabin in May when Dad sold the house. Jamie's parents came and helped us move our things. They have never missed an opportunity to help us with a move, and we've had a lot of moves. When I think of how many people I know that lack supportive and loving family I always take time to thank God that he gave me two supportive and loving families.

Katie and Kevin had bought a place on the river just outside of town, only a mile or so from where my Dad grew up. He used to tell us stories when we were kids of the fun he and his siblings had living along that river. He converted the 2nd story of the big garage/shop at Katie's new place into a very nice little one bedroom apartment and it's where he's been living for the past several months. He bought a pontoon and throughout the summer spent much of his time on the river fishing. He spends a lot of time with his grandkids and great grandkids but he spends quite a lot of time still alone in his apartment missing Mom. We all worry about his health, both physical and emotional. I call him at least once a week and go to visit as often as I can.

Jamie and I are still in our place in Madison. We upgraded our motorhome to a nicer, newer model earlier this summer and have spent almost every weekend taking it somewhere, often times up north to see Dad and the rest of the family. Jamie continues to work hard at his passion in the hotel industry, currently the Director of Revenue and Performance for a hotel management company. He travels often to the many different hotels he helps manage throughout the Midwest.

After years in management, having hundreds of people reporting to me and juggling the chaos that goes with it, I made a pretty big pivot this year when I accepted a new role at my company as the Business Change Manager. I completed my change practitioner certification and spend my days now working on the parts of management I enjoy the most and often had little to no time for in the past. No longer having to manage multiple people, but instead having the privilege of working with those same people on what I like to refer to as "the softer side" of work life. I conduct trainings on how to navigate change in the workplace and balance work life with personal life. I get to create fun group activities designed to help employees feel connected and engaged. I consider myself very lucky to have found my way to this kind of role at this point in my career.

Life without Mom is still fresh and there's not a day that goes by that I don't wish I could pick up the phone and call her. In May, we had plans as an entire family to spend several days at a beautiful 15 bedroom cabin on the water in Eagle River. Originally we would have been celebrating Mom's 70th birthday. We decided to have her burial service the morning before leaving for the get together then use the 4 days away as a family to all be together on Mom's birthday and support each other and make it a celebration of her life. The day of her service I read aloud a eulogy I had written for her. It was as follows:

When I was little, I fell off my bike. I skinned up my knees and my hands. I remember looking at my little red scrapes filled with dirt and gravel and thinking I am never riding this thing again. But then Mom scooped me up and hugged me, took me inside and cleaned me up and before long I was out riding my bike again. I remember liking school for the most part but had bad days like any kid. Mom always knew somehow, and she would hug me, and it was just better. A hug from mom was my cure for most everything growing up. I remember when we lost Marcy, Grandma Simington came out to our house the next day and she walked in and didn't say a word, she just let mom fall into her arms and she hugged her so tight. I remember thinking, oh that's where Mom gets it from. She can hug away pain like her Mom does for her. The last few months of

Mom's life, we were all around a LOT. 24/7, there was never a single moment that at least one of us, but usually most of us, weren't right there with her. It was getting more difficult for her to move around and so I would always insist on letting her stay in her chair when I would hug her hello or goodbye but often she would insist on standing up so she could give me a "real hug". I struggle to remember a single time in my life when Mom didn't put her own needs aside for her kids and her family. Knowing someone like that, who dedicates their life to being the caretaker of everyone else... is such a gift, especially when that someone is your mom. I always looked so forward to her birthday and Mother's day and Christmas, the few times of the year where she tolerated anyone doing something for her. This is a woman whose standard answer to "what do you want for your birthday" was always, "I don't need nothin, just come see me". Mom hugged me when my heart was broken, she hugged me when I accomplished something, she hugged me when we were both happy or both hurting. A few years back, when Dad had heart surgery and we were all so scared, when I finally got to him after traveling across the country for an entire day, I was so relieved to know the doctors said he was going to be ok, but when I saw him with all the machines and lying there... I can barely describe how I felt.. I walked out of that hospital room that day and looked at Mom and she just knew exactly what I was feeling and she was there waiting with open arms. She hugged me and reassured me Dad would be up and about and his old self again before I knew it, and she was right. My mind knows that losing Mom means losing the hug that I need from her now more than ever... but my heart doesn't understand it. In my heart, I just need her to hug me again and make this all better. But if Mom were here right now, I know exactly what she would tell me to do. She'd tell me to lean on Dad, and my siblings, and all these amazing people in this big beautiful family of ours. There are days I ask God why, why did he decide my last hug from Mom would truly be the last. But today I am not going to ask why. I am going to do what Mom would do. She would focus on the things we have to be thankful for. So today, in her honor, in her memory, I am instead going to tell God what I am thankful for, like Mom taught me. Thank you God for my Dad, who was so incredibly loving to my Mother and made her life complete. Thank you God for my brother Nick, whose presence calms me and who has let me cry on his shoulder more times than I can count in the last 6 months. Thank you God for my sister Katie, who, so much like Mom, sets aside her own needs to tend to the rest of us. Thank you God for my sister Jenny, who listens with her whole soul and loves the same. Thank you God for my sister Bobbi, who holds on a little longer with her hugs, just like Mom used to do. Thank you God for the time I had with my sister Marcy, whose energy was so bright and so contagious. Thank you God for my huge extended family. Thank you God for giving me a Mother who taught me that there is so much more than life here on this earth. Thank you God for instilling faith in her that she instilled in me. A faith that helps me stay standing in the midst of so much grief, knowing beyond any doubt that Mom and Marcy are together right now, and that all of us will be together again someday. Every night before going to bed, my parents said a prayer together and every night they ended that prayer the same way; thank you for my husband, thank you for my wife. Today I thank you, God, for choosing them to be my parents. And lastly, I thank you for every precious moment I ever had with this incredible woman, and for every hug she ever gave me that took away every pain I ever had. Thank you God, for my Mom. Amen.

When the service was over we headed for Eagle River in a big caravan of cars. It was a beautiful long weekend and we did our best to make it a happy occasion but inevitably many tears were still shed.

Since her passing we've gained several new members to our already giant family. In late May my nephew Trent got married and we welcomed his wife Carly into our family. In August my nephew Raistlin got married and we welcomed Rebekah. A couple of weeks ago my niece Savanna gave birth to her first child and now little Issic grows our numbers by one more. Last weekend, my nephew Kenny got married and now we get to call Jolisa family too. It may sound like an unusually large amount of events and activity for one family, but not for mine. I buy wedding and new baby cards in bulk these days. Proof that life goes on is the never-ending continuance of the legacy of love that my parents built.

It's harder without Mom, she was at the center of it all, but in our hearts we know she still is. There will be more weddings, more babies, new adventures, and more stories to tell. Mom will forever be at the core of all of them, and we will take the lessons she taught us with us through each of our journeys on this earth. I wish she was here in person, but until we meet again, I know I can close my eyes and see her smiling face and hear her incredible laugh anytime I want. What an amazing woman she was.

Chapter 47

Tomorrow

As I wrap up these pages I am struck by the thought of what's next. With Modern medicine these days, there's a chance my life isn't even half over yet, though I'll need to get more serious about quitting smoking and getting more active and eating healthier if I want that to be true I suppose. I sit here wondering what I might think of the words on these pages 5 years from now, 10 years, 40 years from now. I wonder where I will be in my journey. I wonder how much of what's already happened in my first 40 years will shape the next 40. I wonder as more years go by if I will be inspired to sit down one day and write more of my stories, continued chapters of my life's events, the good, the bad, the triumph, and the heartache.

When I close my eyes and picture what my future might look like, I dream of owning a big beautiful house on the Lake I grew up on, near all my family. It's mine and Jamie's summer home and it's big enough to host massive family get togethers all summer long. We have fun water toys like jet skis and pontoons and kayaks and paddle boats. We have a giant outdoor firepit that can fit our entire families around it for summer nights around the campfire. Every May through September it's our home, during the beautiful summer months in Northern Wisconsin, with the many hours of sunshine that make the days longer and the nights warmer.

In the cold winter months we live somewhere warm and tropical, reminiscent of the times on our beloved Island of St. Croix. We have a beautiful little condo near the ocean and we spend our free time snorkeling, swimming in the turquoise waters, and enjoying a cocktail on our front porch while watching the sunset over the ocean. All our friends and family plan their vacations every year to our little slice of heaven and we become unofficial tour guides/hosts of our tropical paradise multiple times a year as they come for their visits.

I wonder sometimes, will there be a little one in that picture. Will we ever decide to have kids? We talk about it from time to time but neither of us know for sure if that's something we want. We only know we're not in that place today, but not knowing how we'll feel tomorrow is part of what makes life interesting I suppose.

Today I am happy, I have moments of overwhelming sadness when I grieve for those I've lost and long to see again, but I dry my tears and I keep moving forward. Today I have my husband who I love and my dog who I hope will be the first of his kind to live forever. I look out my window and see my nice little neighborhood. All my neighbors are so friendly and we really like it here, though neither of us is looking forward to another Wisconsin winter. Today I have my Dad and I am so thankful, but I worry how much more time I will have with him. Today I have dreams of what the future will bring and what choices we will make next, where we'll go, who we'll meet and how each person and place will change our lives. Today I remind myself to live in the moment and enjoy it. As for what's next... I guess I'll find out tomorrow.

Chapter 48

And Tomorrow...

Seems strange to have another chapter here doesn't it? As I write this, it's now January of 2022. Two months ago when I thought I finished this book, I was so happy with that final line... *"as for what's next... I guess I'll find out tomorrow"*. Seemed a fitting way to wrap up the pages of my life up to this point. Seemed to me that the pain and loss and grief of the past year had settled from a rapid boil to a simmer. I felt as though I had put my pain down on paper and was allowing myself to release it out into the universe. I shared these pages with my siblings first, then more family, then some close extended family and eventually some close friends. I began to get excited about seeing my words in print, in a real book, with a cool cover design and my picture on the back. It's not as though I didn't think anything worth writing about would ever happen to me again, I guess I just felt that I had said what I wanted to say for now.

"Today I have my Dad and I am so thankful, but I worry how much more time I will have with him".

I read those words again today for the first time in over a month. I read those words and chills went down my spine.

To say Dad was struggling adjusting to life without Mom would be an understatement. Don't get me wrong, I was so proud of how hard he had been trying. He was in his new place at my sister Katie's house (a separate apartment steps from her front door). He did his best, especially in the summer months, to keep busy. He'd sold the SUV and bought an old truck that needed work, probably just to give himself something to do. He'd found a great deal on a pontoon and spent quite a bit of time out cruising along the river, fishing and enjoying his old childhood stomping grounds. Still, more often than not, it was obvious that he was still in so much pain over the loss of my Mom.

A couple of months back, he developed an ear infection. At first we thought he'd need some antibiotics and it would clear up and that would be that. But after many weeks, many doctors, many differing opinions, a home pic line, home nurse, and twice daily regimen of my sister (also a nurse) administering powerful antibiotics through an IV, the infection was not seemingly budging. It was clear my Dad's patience with all the doctor's appointments was wearing out.

On Saturday, December 4, 2021 around 4 in the afternoon, I called Dad to check in. He'd been to yet another appointment the day before where they'd done a minor surgery (biopsy), hoping to rule out a cancerous tumor behind the infection. Every time I called Dad this past year our conversation always started the same way. I would say, "Hey Dad, how you doing today?" and he would always say "Oh pretty good Joe, pretty good". On this particular day though, Dad didn't respond with his usual upbeat line. He said slowly and in a somber voice "I've been better". I asked him what was wrong and he said his eye was hurting him terribly. Throughout the entire 10 months since Mom had passed, there was almost no piece of information about Dad I didn't already know before he told me as a result of my siblings and I being overly communicative in our talks and text chats. I knew already that Bobbi had said Dad likely had developed shingles in his eye. Shingles, if you don't know, is sort of an adult version of the chicken pox virus. It is, from what I understand, terribly painful. I pried further with Dad, knowing what he was going to tell me. He explained the shingles and how badly they hurt. I'd never heard him sounding so defeated.

When I hung up the phone with him we'd gotten to a point of him agreeing that he was going to try to eat more for dinner than he did for lunch. His appetite was not great and it was just clear he was in so much pain. I hated hearing him that way and felt it was so unfair. I look back on what I shared in my sibling text chat right after that call and I ask myself why I didn't get in my car and drive up there right then and there. A question I might be stuck asking myself for the rest of my life. I told him I loved him and I was praying hard for him and he told me he loved me too. Below is an excerpt of some of what I sent to my siblings after hanging up the phone:

Just talked to Dad, I wish I understood why on earth this poor man has to deal with so much right now. My hearts just breaking for him right now, I hate all this crap so much.

Bobbi had responded first and agreed with Dad feeling tired of it all and her heart breaking for him too. The others chimed in with agreement based on their most recent interactions with him as well. I shared in my sibling chat another part of my conversation with Dad:

You guys, Dad also said to me, "I just don't want to go to any more appointments Joe, I don't want to", That hit me hard. The way he said it sounded so defeated.

All of us siblings talked back and forth for a bit in our group text about it and all of us were praying hard and feeling frustrated that he was going through all this. The loss of Mom, the unending ear infection, the constant doctor appointments, the differing opinions from all of them, and now a terribly painful bout of shingles, it was just so incredibly unfair. It's not uncommon for one of us siblings to share a prayer in difficult times and as we were wrapping up our conversation this time I shared one:

Lord, please heal our Dad, please. His heart has not yet healed the loss of his wife nor will it likely ever do so but his body is failing him now it seems, and we ask that you restore his physical health and allow him pain-free time to work on his broken heart. It all seems too much so please Lord also help him and those that love him to continue to trust in your timing and your plan, Amen.

Sometimes, when we pray for something and it doesn't happen exactly the way we asked for in our prayer, it can shake our faith. Difficult things in life like loss, heartache, disease, natural disasters... all things that can shake our faith. I prayed the prayer above throughout Saturday afternoon and evening, thinking of Dad and hoping he was feeling better, having some relief from the pain and getting his appetite back. I prayed and I prayed. *Lord help him trust in your timing, help me trust in your timing.* Why did I focus on that part so much, why was I so concerned about Dad trusting in God's timing? What happened next certainly makes it seem like I prayed those specific words because I somehow knew what was coming, but I can assure you, there was absolutely no part of me that could have known what was coming.

Jamie and I had gone to bed earlier than usual Saturday night. Normally we allow ourselves to stay up a bit later on Saturdays because we have no obligations on Sundays and can sleep in a bit. This Sunday was different though as Jamie would be heading out of state for work for a few days and needing to leave Mid-morning on Sunday. How quickly his plans changed. How quickly our lives changed... again, just like that, in an instant, on the other side of a phone call.

I woke around 7am and reached to shut off my alarm. After hitting the button on top my alarm clock several times with the alarm still sounding I realized it wasn't my alarm, it was my phone, ringing. I opened my eyes, groggy and confused, trying to think what day it was and picked up my phone to see Kevin Klein was calling. Kevin, my sister Katie's husband. A man of few words, kind, quiet, hard working. He was and is one of my favorite people on this planet. He's a good man, a good Dad, a good husband to my sister whom I adore. What he wasn't, however, is someone who had ever called me on the phone. To my knowledge, I can't recall a time when I'd ever picked up my phone to see Kevin calling me.

It was Sunday morning. It was 7am. Kevin was calling me.

I was groggy and just waking up, but I knew before I answered that something was wrong. What waited on the other end of that call would, for the first time in many years, be something powerful enough to shake my faith.

I don't recall much of anything that happened after I said "Hello" and Kevin said, "Joe, I am so sorry to have to tell you this, your Dad shot himself, he died Joe, I'm so sorry".

Chapter 49

... And Tomorrow

Jamie has since filled me in a bit on the details of that morning. He tells me I screamed, began sobbing, told him what Kevin had just told me, and threw my phone on the floor.

I don't remember any of that.

He says I fell out of the bed and he raced over to my side and held me and we both cried together. I guess we each packed a bag of clothes and I went upstairs to pack up some things for our dog, who would be later picked up by Jamie's parents. Jamie called them to tell them what happened and arrange for that.

I don't remember that either.

Jamie tells me he came into the kitchen to find me standing there with a blank stare on my face and suddenly I picked up an un-opened 12 pack of canned soda, screamed out "why does everything always have to be on his f*cking terms?!" and threw the soda across the room, causing cans to explode and be strewn about.

Surely I would remember that. I don't.

It's so very strange to me to know that I could do something like that and have absolutely no memory of it. I remember seeing the cans on the floor before we left the house that morning, I recall having no idea how they'd gotten there and wondering what on earth caused such a mess.

The days that followed were awful. Learning the details of the morning, what my sister went through. Sitting with my siblings in shock and anger and sobbing. Trying to figure out who to tell and what to tell them. Being thrust for the 2nd time in a matter of months, into planning a funeral for a parent. Phone calls, visits from family and friends, tears and more tears. Tremendous guilt over asking my sister Jenny to write Dad's eulogy. I had written Mom's and part of me felt like it was so wrong of me not to also write Dad's, but I couldn't do it. Jenny wrote a beautiful tribute to Dad and read it aloud at his burial service. I especially loved what she wrote about the things he left us:

> With Nick, he left a selfless strength and compassion that always protects and leads.
>
> With Kate, he left a deep love for family combined with a witty and welcoming spirit.
>
> With me [Jen], he left a desire to celebrate the good things even in the midst of the struggle.
>
> With Bobbi, he left a gentleness of heart and a powerful empathy for those who are hurting.

With Joe, he left a brilliant sense of humor and an ability to evoke healing laughter in just the right way, at just the right moment.

Grief is a powerful and awful beast of a thing. It's hard enough to navigate one devastating loss, much less two in the same year. I find myself more often than not these days in a kind of fog. It's hard to describe, but I heard a song recently wherein the chorus it says "You and I both know, the house is haunted, you and I both know, the ghost is me". Those words resonated with me. How true that my home is indeed haunted by the ghost of who I was. Who I was before Mom got sick, who I was before the doctor told us that day that they'd tried to save her but she was gone. Who I was before Kevin told me Dad took matters into his own hands. Who I was before I buried both my parents.

That person I was, he's not me anymore and I'm not him. Maybe that's ok, maybe that's how it's supposed to be. Tragedy changes a person, not always for the better and not always for the worse, but nevertheless it changes you. We are powerless to stop it and yet we spend so much time fighting internally with ourselves to "get back to normal". Everyone around me keeps saying things like "take it one day at a time, you will be back to your old self eventually". The thing is, I won't. I can't be that ghost of who I once was. I can't because that person existed in a world where his Mom hadn't died suddenly and his Dad hadn't taken his own life. The world I live in is not the same now. I am not the same now.

A dear friend of mine sent me a book called "Permission to Mourn" by Tom Zuba. To be honest, I wasn't really ready to read anything that might be considered self-help when it arrived. On a recent morning though, I was up early, Jamie was still asleep, and the house was quiet. The book was sitting on the stand next to my chair in the living room and I picked it up intending to read the back cover and maybe the foreword. Instead, I read the entire book cover to cover in just under an hour. I couldn't put it down. How articulate this Mr. Zuba was in his way of describing almost exactly what I was feeling. Chapter 4, page 19, there were the words *"You try to look and act "normal" hoping and praying that one day you'll actually feel normal again. And people tell you how strong you are. How "good" you are doing. How great it is to have the old "you" back. But you know a different truth. You feel numb. Empty. Lethargic. Hopeless. Exhausted."*

The book would go on to dig into my very soul and describe things I had struggled to find words for but knew I was feeling. Though my heart ached for Mr. Zuba and the tremendous amount of shocking and unexpected losses he'd been through in his life, I found myself feeling so thankful for his words. His words that he'd never have written had he not experienced such loss, such grief. I'm sure, given the chance, he'd trade the book he wrote for all his loved ones back. Of course he would. I would. Anyone would. But life is about finding triumph in the midst of tragedy. Life is about finding a way to use your pain and your hurt and your grief to pull someone else back up off the ground. We tell our stories and we share our losses with others and maybe they recognize a little piece of themselves in our story. So today and probably tomorrow, and for quite some time I am going to give myself permission to mourn, as the book says. I didn't just lose my Mom and Dad, I lost a sense of security. I lost, for now at least, most of myself. Who I knew myself to be, how I approached life and relationships. I can't find that same guy right now. I feel mostly like I am on some sort of grief auto-pilot. Life doesn't stop and wait for us to conquer our grief, we have to keep putting one foot in front of the other in the interim. We have to go back to work. We have to pay the bills. We have to run errands. We don't get a free pass to simply shut down.

Tomorrow and tomorrow and tomorrow, why did I choose to label the last few chapters this way? If you're familiar with Shakespeare then you know I stole the line from MacBeth. Macbeth's tomorrow and tomorrow and tomorrow speech is in response to the news that Lady Macbeth is dead; and to him, this signifies the beginning of the end for him. The truth is, I never dreamed these chapters would be something I would ever write. Chapters so painful because within them I will, for the first time, admit what I have been afraid to say; Dad took his own life because he didn't see a purpose in continuing on without Mom. Yes, he was in pain. Yes, he was losing his patience with his failing physical health. Yes, he may have been in so much physical pain that he was not of his right mind. After all, how could he leave us that way if he took any time to think it through? How could he do this knowing his daughter would find him and never be able to unsee the things she saw that morning? Dad would never do that to her... to us. The plain truth is that Dad would have endured, gone to more appointments, fought for answers, grinned and bared the pain if he knew it meant more time with Mom. I believe that in my heart of hearts.

Dad was wrong. The loss of his wife didn't have to be the beginning of the end for him. Dad tried, we all tried. But in the end, Dad made his choice. I will find a way, eventually, to forgive him for that choice. After all, I know just how much I lost when Mom died, but I can't begin to understand the depth of what he lost that day. I miss him, I loved him dearly, but I think I am going to be angry for a few more tomorrows.

Chapter 50

One Day

I hold onto the printed pages of this book. The book that used to end at chapter 47. The book I gave to Dad and asked him to read. His copy is still dog-eared at page 99, just before the start of Chapter 23, that's as far as he got. He told me it was hard for him to read because so much of it made him emotional.

My Dad's generation largely considered a man getting emotional to be a bad thing from what I've learned over the years. The last time I had asked him about the book was a couple of weeks before he died. He told me he'd only made it to page 20 at that time but when I found the copy in his apartment it was clear he'd read much more. It made me happy to know the last chapter he read was about our dog Georgie. My dad loved Georgie and his face always lit up when he'd see him.

I miss him. I am not sure how to describe the feeling of being almost 40 and feeling like an orphan. It's bizarre, uncomfortable, and more than anything... it's lonely.

One day, I will forgive him. One day I will find a way to harness all my grief into something productive. One day, I hope to find a way to help others through their sorrows by calling upon my own. One day, all this pain and hurt and anger will not be so all consuming. One day I might start to feel whole again.

I hope and I pray each night that the day will be tomorrow but each new day comes and I still feel broken. The truth is, I may not ever feel whole again, and maybe that's ok. Maybe my "one day" won't be about feeling whole again, maybe my "one day" will be about learning to love the broken pieces of myself and continuing forward, triumphant even.

Last night I had a dream that Dad and I were walking along the gravel roads of Mudbrook. A truck suddenly slid past us and came to a stop sideways as we both realized the road was suddenly covered in thick layers of snow and ice. As I turned toward Dad to ask him what we should do, I realized he was now about 100 yards back, standing in the middle of the road. His back was to me, holding his hand up in the air, as if to signal to oncoming traffic that they should stop. I could see several more cars coming and each one was now sliding sideways. I screamed out to Dad to get out of the road but he couldn't hear me. I tried to run toward him but my legs were so heavy and slow. I woke up in a cold sweat, out of breath, and terrified. Dad was in danger. I couldn't save him.

I don't know what's next. I suppose none of us really do. Here's what I do know. I know the love of a big family is more powerful than anything on this earth. I know if you scream at the top of your lungs while alone in your car it can be very freeing. I know my Dad

237

loved me, my Mom loved me, and I loved them. I know, one day, I will see them again. I know that I am ready to let go now, send this book, these words, out into the world for anyone to read. It's honest, it's often painful, but it's my life, and I am ready to share it now.

Made in the USA
Monee, IL
13 May 2023

33644337R00134